Teaching with the Internet

Cherry Sparks

Teacher Created Materials, Inc.

Cover Design by Darlene Spivak

Made in U.S.A.

ISBN 1-57690-475-X

Order Number TCM 2475

www.teachercreated.com

Table of Contents

Introduction

There is much excitement generated by this thing called the Internet. Using computers and telecommunications enhances communication skills, encourages children to express ideas, motivates children to move forward in learning, and opens new worlds to explore. When children are excited about learning, great things happen. Educators and parents note profound changes in attitude and achievement. When children discover the many worlds online and the speed at which they can be part of these worlds, they are intrigued and eager to jump into action.

On the information superhighway there are resources that integrate the speeding visual culture our children are used to with traditional academic learning. These resources can bring busy families together and encourage participation. They invite exploration and adventure. They are educational, and they are fun!

This book is not so much an instructional manual but more a guide for educators to use to journey with students across the globe at the touch of a button. This book will provide an in-depth look at the rationale for the use of technology, specifically the Internet. It will describe steps for implementing a telecommunications program in the classroom with specific examples along the way. The journey through cyberspace is an exciting one. Enjoy!

Coming to Terms

In a letter from Vice President Al Gore:

"The development of a National and Global Information infrastructure will advance the way we live, work, learn and share information with each other here in the United States and around the world. Communications technologies will play a critical role in a global economy that is ever more dependent upon information for expanded business and trade opportunities.

These opportunities must extend to our children. This nation cannot tolerate, nor can we afford, a society in which our children lack access to information. President Clinton and I recognize this fact, and we are working to make sure children have access to the Information Superhighway. We want to help American children achieve dominance in math and science, school to work transition, and basic problem solving skills by guaranteeing the best schools, teachers, and courses possible without regard to geography, distance, resources, or disability.

Thomas Jefferson said that information is the currency of democracy. Through our support of the Information Superhighway, we will work to make American democracy richer."

> This nation cannot tolerate, nor can we afford, a society in which our children lack access to information.

What Is the Internet?

It is difficult to define the Internet in a few sentences. Technically, the Internet is a global network made up of millions of interconnected computers. It is a spider-like system of millions of computer networks. What makes the Internet so incredibly powerful is that these computers store an extraordinary amount of information which is accessible from any computer connected to the Internet. This information is different from that stored in print media in a couple of ways. First of all, the information is stored, transmitted, and received digitally, which means that it can be accessed in a number of different forms, including text, video, and audio. Second, the Internet is interactive, which means that the information you receive is a result of the selections you make.

Educators have a responsibility to students to teach them about the Internet.

With the Internet, the possibilities are endless—school children in Japan can talk to their new friends in Arizona. Teachers and administrators can have a conference with other colleagues thousands of miles away. A professor on a business trip can access the computer in her home or office and then dispatch many messages with a few simple clicks. And these are just the beginnings. With the Internet, the only limits are the ones you set. Educators have a responsibility to students to teach them about the Internet. Doing so can change your perspective on global teaching.

Where Did It Come From?

The United States military laid the foundation for the Information Superhighway in the late 1960s as a global, fail-safe communications network designed to continue to operate even if one or more links became inoperative. Universities and research laboratories were granted Internet access when they began to do more business with the government. Funded mostly by government money, the Internet was used exclusively by the government, research institutions, and colleges and universities for twenty years.

In early 1992, policies regulating the commercial use of the Internet were relaxed, allowing unrestricted use for commercial purposes. As a result, commercial traffic on the Internet is growing rapidly.

The operating philosophy of the Internet is that of a free sharing of information. Most of the universities, libraries, schools, government agencies, and even most businesses which are online allow users access to their information at no cost. No one owns the Internet—the costs of operations are shared jointly by its users, educational organizations, government research agencies, the military, and commercial organizations.

What Is the Web?

The World Wide Web (WWW) is not the same thing as the Internet. The World Wide Web is an interactive, graphical presentation of information on the Internet. The Web is part of the Internet—the most widely used and the most accessible part of the Internet. The good news is that due to the ease of use, one does not have to be a computer guru to use the resources available on the Web. Young children can use the Web with just a few simple instructions.

Cyberspace

Cyberspace is the place where people and computer meet. It is not a physical location that you can touch or visit. It is another dimension, but reachable and at your fingertips with your computer. The word cyberspace was originally used by science-fiction writer William Gibson and has since become part of our everyday language.

You can't touch the Internet, and this intangibility confuses many beginning users. The Internet is about *how* resources are linked and *what* resources are available.

How Big Is the Internet?

It is very difficult to measure the number of computers on the Internet because so many computers are connected to networks that are connected to the Internet. It is safe to estimate that as many as 50 million people use the Internet on a regular basis. If the number of people signing onto the Internet continued to grow at its current rate, every person on the planet would be on the Internet by the year 2003!

Nobody knows for sure how big the Internet is or how many networks are actually linked, but there are sites on every continent, including Antarctica. New user sites are continually being added. The Internet has grown at an exponential rate since its beginning. It is the largest network of computers in the world and is growing at about ten percent each month.

There are millions of computers that provide data on the Net, and that number seems to be changing hourly. Colleges and universities, research organizations, government entities, and businesses are all rushing to find ways to connect to and sometimes exploit Internet resources. Schools are no exception. Schools are not only consuming information, they are producing it.

How Does the Internet Work?

The Web has a hypermedia system. This means that a click on any

It is safe to estimate that as many as 50 million people use the Internet on a regular basis.

link may take you to another related source in the form of sound, graphic, or text file. The first universal interface is the World Wide Web. The Web makes it unnecessary to think about where the things you want are located. You do not need to know that the file you want is in Sydney, Australia, or the path to the director where it resides. Geographic regions and intellectual spheres disappear, giving the illusion that a library of knowledge is at your fingertips by way of your keyboard and the click of your mouse.

To view information at a Web site, both a Web browser and a URL (Universal Resource Locator) are needed. A Web browser is software that displays the graphics and text of a specified site. The URL is a special kind of address that tells the Web browser what site to go to. For example, to access today's news at *CNN*, we need to know the address:

http://www.cnn.com

The first part of the address, *http*, is the protocol which is used to transfer data over the Internet. The http protocol stands for HyperText Transfer Protocol. The two slashes following the colon indicate that what follows is an Internet address, in this case *www.cnn.com*. The *www* indicates that the address is on the World Wide Web, *cnn* is the host name, and *com* is a domain identifier that indicates a commercial organization. Note that URL addresses do not contain spaces.

Most Web sites are divided into Web pages with one page designated as the home page. The home page, which may be thought of as a table of contents for that site, often contains links to other pages at that site and can contain links to other Web sites. These links, called *hyperlinks,* appear as underlined or colored words or as a special graphic on the page. Clicking on a hyperlink displays a different Web page or part of the current page if it is a long one. The newly displayed page can also contain hyperlinks. Clicking on hyperlinks to go from Web site to Web site is called *surfing* the Web. For example, at the *USA Today* site, clicking on the movie reviews hyperlink takes us from the home page to a page containing movie reviews. From the movie reviews we could click on a hyperlink that takes us to the Web site of the movie studio producing our selected movie. You may even be able to go to a site which lists showtimes at theatres in your neighborhood. And if you aren't sure where the theater is located, you can find on the Internet a map with directions from your home to the theater.

You can follow hypertext links between Web pages according to your whim or according to your research needs. Because many links are not always straightforward and you may not be sure where that link will lead, there is a great possibility for getting lost in the Web. There are no rules that prevent people who create Web pages from making whatever links they want.

Finding the sites of most interest to you will take a little time and probably a lot of browsing.

The Growth of the Web in Schools

Seldom have we seen the depth and breadth of infatuation with information technology since the advent of the World Wide Web. A veritable frenzy of interest and action on the Web has caused an explosive growth of Web servers around the world, including education sites. Given current trends in local, state, and federal initiatives to wire our nation's schools, we can only expect this trend to accelerate.

Unlike so many previous educational innovations and fads promoted by educational experts, regular classroom teachers who have tested these waters have become convinced that the Web is one of those rare technologies that will have a transformational impact on learning both in and out of school. The Internet is not seen as a passive tool which simply delivers information but rather as a dynamic, participatory medium which promotes a unique style of learning that emphasizes resources, relationships, and exploration.

What Is Next?

The Internet is in its infancy. Five or six years ago, few people knew what it was, yet today, millions of people access the Internet daily. As the Internet grows and matures, more and more people will make use of its resources to find information, perform financial transactions, go shopping—the possibilities are limitless! Undoubtedly, one of the primary uses of the Internet will be in education.

"In the United States, education is the means by which all children—rich or poor—acquire the tools they need to rise as high as their dreams and effort will take them. Properly harnessed, technology will lift those dreams even higher by quite literally bringing the world into our living rooms. A research project for a civics class that once required a plane ticket to Washington, for example, can now be completed through the resources available on the Internet. A computer and a modem will transport students to the greatest museums in America and Europe without leaving their homes. Students who travel the Internet have the same access to Presidential statements and speeches as the reporters who travel at great expense in the White House press pool" (Bob Kerrey, United States Senator, state of Nebraska).

The Internet is not seen as a passive tool which simply delivers information but rather as a dynamic, participatory medium which promotes a unique style of learning that emphasizes resources, relationships, and exploration.

5

Importance to Educators

Teachers who weave
the Internet into their
curriculums to teach
students how to use
the network to find
and use information to
reach a goal turn
students into
independent learners
rather than passive
listeners.

The Internet is the fastest growing communications medium ever! Many schools from kindergarten through grade 12 are part of this explosive growth. This is important because schools which use the Internet do not simply bring students into the future of information technology—they turn their students into something education reformers have been talking about for years—lifelong learners!

Teachers who weave the Internet into their curriculums to teach students how to use the network to find and use information to reach a goal turn students into independent learners rather than passive listeners. Besides teaching students to search for, find, and use information, they bring students into contact with people they would never meet otherwise. While the Internet is comprised of tons of information, it is also made up of people of all races, creeds, cultures, and colors, and they all have personal stories and knowledge to share. Because the culture of the Internet is one of free sharing of information, busy professionals, worldwide renowned experts, and countless others dispense their knowledge with no expectation of payment, except maybe thanks. That in itself is a worthy lesson for young people.

The typical classroom is no longer bound by four walls but is open to include students, experts, and learning experiences from around the world. The Internet is changing the *way* students learn, *when* they learn, *where* they learn, and *who* teaches them.

Because the Internet contains so many resources, both information and people, the Web is an ideal medium for helping to gather and process much of the raw information for a student project. There is nothing new about projects. Good teachers have always used project-based learning as a supplement to their regular course of instruction. Any teacher who has taken a group on a field trip, had students enter a project in a science fair, had a class garden, or any one of a thousand activities that involve students in studying the real world around them has conducted a project-based learning activity.

A review of current literature on educational reform identifies a number of important qualities of improved learning that schools should strive to achieve. The SCANS Report (Secretary's Commission on Achieving Necessary Skills) maintains that in addition to basic language and computational literacy, high school graduates must master the abilities to organize resources; work with others; locate, evaluate, and use information; understand complex work systems; and work with a variety of technologies.

Effective Internet projects encourage students to work on a problem in depth rather than covering many topics superficially.

Learning to Learn

Effective Internet projects encourage students to work on a problem in depth rather than covering many topics superficially. Students also engage in *just in time learning,* learning what is needed to solve a problem or complete a project rather than working in a preset curriculum sequence. Both of these strategies are cited in educational reform literature as being important tools to improve learning.

Lifelong Learning

Internet projects build learning experiences on the kind of learning one does throughout life rather than only on "school" subjects. By using the real tools for intellectual work that are used in the workplace, rather than oversimplified textbook techniques, students become familiar with the kinds of knowledge that exist. Finding information and people on the Internet gives students the ability to acquire the information they may need.

Multicultural Education

With the Internet, teachers can make student projects global affairs. Teachers match students with e-mail pen pals anywhere in the world to collect weather data, to learn about world cultures, or to practice a foreign language with native speakers. Students can join a global project to correspond with explorers in the Central American jungles. They can invite a writer to visit them electronically to exchange questions and answers.

Effective use of the Internet makes it feasible to connect students and teachers for national and international exchanges. These links enable students from very different backgrounds to construct cultural bridges by investigating common issues from different perspectives. As an example, consider seventh grade students from Wichita, Kansas, discussing the rationale for the actions leading to the events of the Boston Tea Party with a group of seventh graders from Birmingham, England.

Active Learning

All of us learn best by doing. In a well-designed Internet project, students gather information and data, explore, create, experiment, and organize information. They have access to people and information from the real world and develop a closer relationship to the real world context of problems and projects. The connections to real people, events, and problems in the world bring a relevance and connection that are immediate and involve their interest, their intellect, and their participation.

Cooperative Learning

Cooperative learning encourages active engagement by the students in learning, and it also builds critical skills needed in today's workplace. Internet projects vastly widen the audience and opportunity for cooperative learning by involving and communicating with a wide cross section of people around the world. Students work directly with people from other places and cultures, and they collaborate not only with peers but with mentors and experts in a large number of fields.

Telecommunications provide many opportunities for students to work cooperatively both within their own classes and groups comprised of students at different schools. Teachers who have implemented cooperative learning with technology supported activities endorse it; research supports the use of group interactions to promote positive social interchanges and increase instructional effectiveness.

Collaborative problem solving holds the richest potential for the use of the Internet as a tool to support constructivist learning. Students engage in activities that combine collecting information with interpersonal communication to respond to curriculum-based challenges. The Internet transports these activities beyond the classroom walls and creates a virtual community in which students construct learning.

Collaborative problem solving holds the richest potential for the use of the Internet as a tool to support constructivist learning.

Personalization

Students learn best when their learning and activities relate to things which they can identify with personally and when they work on projects and problems of intrinsic interest to themselves. When students are involved in developing a learning project, they assume more ownership of both the process and the outcome. The wealth of people and resources available on the Internet can cater to any appropriate interest students wish to pursue.

Internet use inspires students (and educators) by making learning exciting and relevant. Students find it motivating to correspond with peers and experts who would be inaccessible through other means. The literature abounds with articles about students getting "turned on" to learning through telecommunications.

Computers and networks do not pre-judge people on the basis of their race, physical abilities, or appearance. Many shy or self-conscious students have blossomed through the anonymity of using the Internet.

Individualization

Research clearly demonstrates that different people learn best in different ways. See Howard Gardner's *Theory of Multiple Intelligences* for more information. Students learn best when the material and teaching applications are customized to respond to these individual differences in learning styles and cognitive strengths. Internet projects and communication on the Internet help to support individualization.

Communication Skills

The Internet can enhance learning by providing unique opportunities for students to practice, demonstrate, and critique written communication skills. Communicating online is quite a different experience from communicating in person.

Students soon learn to be explicit and sharpen their skills in order to get their points across to peers in other cities and countries. Telecommunications offer a forum for students to share their stories and manuscripts. Many educators have been impressed by the effort students put into their writings when the students realize their work will be shared with their peers in other schools.

> The Internet can enhance learning by providing unique opportunities for students to practice, demonstrate, and critique written communication skills.

Students throughout the world can communicate daily about lifestyles, politics, careers, and so on. Messages can be sent to hundreds of people throughout the world within a few seconds. Users are not dependent on the reliability or schedules of postal services. Although it is certainly possible for students to exchange letters via regular mail service, the Internet is usually more meaningful because the feedback is fast and immediate, allowing the students to stay focused on their ideas, projects, and interchanges. There are endless possibilities. The challenge for teachers is to structure this exciting, sometimes overwhelming, resource into their students' everyday lives.

Many schools have participated in programs that provide online access to experts on science, language, technology, or other areas. Online conferences are also a good avenue to contact experts in specific fields. For example, Pitsco's Ask-an-Expert Web site (*http://www.askanexpert.com/askanexpert/*) provides access to experts in more than three hundred fields.

Up-to-Date Information

After a book is written, it may take a year or longer before it is printed and becomes available in bookstores and libraries. CD-ROM technology provides a wealth of information, but the discs are usually updated only on an annual or quarterly basis. The best means to access current information is through the Internet. Some services, e.g., weather, stock market prices, and sports scores, are revised almost constantly, providing up-to-the minute information.

Personal and Professional Development

Teachers often feel intellectually isolated in their classrooms with little time or opportunity to interact with their peers. Through the use of the Internet, educators can easily and inexpensively continue their professional growth by interacting with others through e-mail or special-interest conferences. Telecommunications and distance learning also reduce the isolation felt by both students and teachers in rural communities.

The Internet and telecommunications technology are changing our world in profound ways. The way we communicate, work, and learn is fundamentally different, and educators must be prepared.

Teachers often feel intellectually isolated in their classrooms with little time or opportunity to interact with their peers.

School Internet Trouble Spots and Solutions

One of the primary reasons that the Internet is not connected to every classroom in every school is cost, but without the Internet, the cost to the students' futures may be higher. The initial cost of computers, phone lines, connections, and providers may seem high to a school district already managing on tight funds, but these costs can be reduced. Recently, the wiring of schools on Net Days and the E-Rate enable schools to get online with minimum costs.

One of the primary reasons that the Internet is not connected to every classroom in every school is cost, but without the Internet, the cost to the students' futures may be higher.

Available Internet Tools

E-Mail, Listservs, and Newsgroups

One of the joys of getting involved in online telecommunications is discovering new ways to create exciting, productive learning experiences. Educators can tap into dozens, even hundreds, of resources that will help implement telecommunications in the curriculum.

When it comes to K–12 instructional material of all kinds, computer oriented or not, there is no shortage on the Internet. Lesson plans come online every day in new places. There are sites for enormous collections of lesson plans, information sharing, ideas, documents, current research, government, businesses, national and international organizations, museums, and more.

Electronic Mail (E-Mail)

By far the most exciting use of the Internet is people-to-people connections. Electronic mail (e-mail), the most common use of the Internet, is very easy to use. E-mail is any message sent over a network. It could stay in the school's local area network, or it could pass through an Internet service provider to the outback in Australia.

By using e-mail, students and teachers can exchange ideas with people all over the planet. It is awesome to think that through the power of the Internet, you or your students can communicate directly with everyone from research scientists to movie stars. Using e-mail is a good place to begin exploration of the Internet from your classroom.

E-mail is versatile and easy. Students can send a letter to a local politician about the curfew recently imposed or a letter to a best friend who is in another state. By using e-mail, you can reach virtually everyone on the Internet. The letter arrives almost instantaneously and can be copied and forwarded to lots of different people with just a click of a button.

Electronic mail is so popular primarily because it is easy to understand and use. It is quick, efficient, and fun. Addresses for electronic mail messages usually follow these patterns:

username@location.domain

Janedoe@anyschool.edu
President@whitehouse.gov

The username (the first letters and numbers to the left of the @ symbol) is generally assigned to you by your Internet service provider. Depending on the size of your organization, sometimes usernames can get lengthy. An @ sign separates the username from the location and domain. Examples of location names are WHITEHOUSE and LOC (Library of Congress). Domain names are COM for a commercial organization, EDU for an educational organization, GOV for government organization, ORG for an organization, and NET for an Internet provider. Computer names are usually the names of servers. Put these parts together with the proper punctuation, and you have an Internet address. Be careful to use the exact punctuation. The last few letters, referred to as the domain, are separated from the computer's name by a period and will help you determine what kind of organization sent the mail and, in some cases, the country of origin. Notice that there are no spaces between any parts of an Internet address and that some parts are separated by periods.

Because the Internet works in a standard protocol (common language), virtually any computer can send and receive e-mail. E-mail has two parts, the header and the message. The header may contain information about you, the sender, the receiver's electronic address, the date, and a subject. The message part contains your

Because the Internet works in a standard protocol (common language), virtually any machine can send and receive e-mail.

13

birthday wishes, your request for information about a vacation to Cancun, or whatever! You can print, reply, forward, redirect, or save your message by using commands from the pulldown menus at the top of the screen.

E-mail is your personal connection to the Internet which you and your students can use to send messages to just one other person or to a big group of people. Check your e-mail instructions on how to set up your address book and group mail. Students can make friends very quickly on the Internet and may begin to receive many messages every day.

To get an idea of just how useful e-mail can be in a classroom to gather information, have students generate a list of ten common foods they like and create a short e-mail survey designed to be used to compare prices. Send the survey via e-mail to a teacher you know on the Internet and ask that teacher's students to price each item and return the results via e-mail.

The Internet brings to teachers and their students resources, tools, worldwide contacts, and challenging projects.

Making contacts around the world through e-mail can make many projects more interesting. Students are encouraged to work cooperatively while seeking and sharing information beyond the classroom. They can exchange several letters with Internet pen pals in the same amount of time that it would take for a regularly mailed letter to make a one-way trip.

The Internet brings to teachers and their students resources, tools, worldwide contacts, and challenging projects. The constraints of time and space are not relevant on the Internet. The Internet can provide teachers with access to old friends and help them make new contacts. Teacher isolation becomes a thing of the past. Ideas are updated often, and new information is distributed to Internet users very quickly.

Through e-mail, parents and teachers can communicate directly. Teachers can send messages and assignments to children who are connected online at home.

For classroom teachers as well as administrators, telecommunications can serve as managerial and organizational tools. In most e-mail systems, messages can be grouped and stored in electronic folders for easy retrieval. In addition, school records, such as attendance and grades, can be easily and quickly transmitted between institutions. Electronic messages can be sent any time of the day or night, thus eliminating phone tag.

Educators can utilize the many free educational resources on the Internet in their teaching and preparation of teaching materials. For instance, teachers may find free computer software to help students learn a concept or skill.

Mailing Lists (Listservs)

A mailing list (or a listserv) is a special e-mail situation where messages are sent from one person to everyone who has subscribed to or become part of a group. When anyone in the group posts a message to the listserv, you can send a message back to just that person or to the entire listserv.

The advantage of a subscription via e-mail is that it is free. Some organizations distribute their newsletters via e-mail. This way, they can avoid the printing and mailing costs and "subscribers" receive the news almost instantly.

The other common use for a listserv is as a discussion group on virtually any topic you can imagine: hobbies, occupations, politics, trends, etc.

One serious drawback of listservs is that it is easy to become overwhelmed by the vast number of e-mail messages you receive each day from the group.

The advantage of a subscription via e-mail is that it is free.

You can find a variety of interesting telecommunications projects at the KIDLINK listserv. Send an e-mail subscribe message to LISTSERV@ndsuvml.bit. The message text should read as follows: subscribe KIDLINK (your name).

The *Global Classroom Discussion List* offers a discussion of online projects and ideas with a decidedly international flavor. Send an e-mail subscribe message to LISTSERV@uriacc.uri.edu. The message text should read as follows: subscribe GC-L (your name).

Newsgroups are sometimes called bulletin boards. A newsgroup is an electronic version of a corkboard model in which you might post a message asking if anyone has any good ideas for teaching keyboarding skills to your students. After a few days, you will have several replies to your question.

USENET, the collective name for all newsgroups, is like a huge collection of electronic bulletin board systems. An international medium for debate and information exchange, it is the Internet's open discussion forum.

USENET is made up of thousands of electronic discussion forums called newsgroups. Each newsgroup is composed of a series of electronic messages (called articles) on the themes of a given topic. The topic can be anything from stamp collecting to nuclear physics to block scheduling to pets to computer software. The article themes (known as threads) can be anything related to those topics.

You can read the articles in any newsgroup and respond to them by sending e-mail to the article's author (known as the poster). In most newsgroups, you can also respond by posting a follow-up, that is, by publishing your own article. Additionally, you can start your own discussion or propose a topic for an entirely new newsgroup.

To access newsgroups you need a software program called a news reader. Most Web browsers, including *Internet Explorer* and *Netscape Navigator,* include a news reader built in. There are an estimated 30,000 newsgroups covering just about any topic you can imagine, with more being added every day.

Newsgroups are different from mailing lists in that the messages you read are not sent to your mailbox. Instead, they are sent to a community mailbox.

There are an estimated 30,000 newsgroups covering just about any topic you can imagine, with more being added every day.

MAILING LISTS

SOME EDUCATIONAL MAILING LISTS

BILINGUE-L
Developmental bilingual elementary education list
Address: listserv@Reynolds.k12.or.us

CHILDRENS-VOICE
Publishes writing from children ages 5–14
Address: listproc@scholnet.carleton.ca

COSNDISC
Consortium for School Networking
Address: listproc@yukon.cren.org

ECENET-L
Early childhood education list
Address: listserv@uiucvmd.bitnet

EDINFO-L
Contains information related to educational issues
Address: edinfo-l@iubvm.ucs.indiana.edu

EDTECH
Information on educational technology
Address: listserv@msu.edu

ELEMUG
Elementary School Users' Group
Address: listserv@uicvm.uic.edu

GRANTS-L
NSF grants information list
Address: listserv@onondaga.bitnet

IECC
Intercultural E-Mail Classroom Connections
Address: iecc-request@stolaf.edu

K12-AUP
Acceptable use policies discussion
Address: k12-aup-request@merit.edu

Reprinted from TCM 668 Internet for Teachers & Parents, *Teacher Created Materials,* 1996.

SOME EDUCATIONAL MAILING LISTS *(cont.)*

KIDLINK
Activity projects for kids
Address: listserv@vm1.nodak.edu

KIDOPEDIA
About creation of the Kidopedia sites around the world and related issues
Address:listserv@sjuvm.stjohns.edu

KIDSPHERE
International kid's dialog
Address: kidsphere-request@vms.cis.pitt.edu

MATHSED-L
Discussion group on mathematics in education
Address: listserv@deakin.edu.au

MEDIA-L
Focuses on the role of the media in education
Address: listserv@bingvmb.cc.binghamton.edu

MIDDLE-L
Discussion of middle school-aged children
Address: listserv@vmd.cso.uiuc.edu

MMEDIA-L
Discussions of multimedia in education
Address: listserv@vmtecmex.bitnet

MUSIC-ED
Music education discussion
Address: listserv@artsedge.kennedy-center.org

NARST-L
Focuses on teaching science; sponsored by the National Association for Research in Science Teaching
Address: listserv@uwf.bitnet

TAG-L
A talented and gifted list
Address: Listserv@ndsuvm1.nodak.edu

UAARTED
Art education discussion
Address: listserv@arizvm1.bitnet

Reprinted from TCM 668 Internet for Teachers & Parents, *Teacher Created Materials,* 1996.

E-Mail Project Ideas

The most popular type of educational telecomputing activity is one in which individuals talk electronically to other individuals, individuals talk to groups, or groups talk to other groups. Communicating with keypals is probably the most common telecomputing activity, similar in form to surface mail pen pal activities. Student-to-student keypal exchanges involve more managerial work than many teachers have time for and often diverge from the chosen topic of study. Group-to-group exchanges, especially those with a particular study emphasis, can evolve into fascinating cultural explorations without overwhelming activity facilitators with the transfer and processing of e-mail. Keypal activities are also perfect conduits for language study. Keypal projects often combine the use of newer and traditional media.

Many keypal projects emphasize the importance of students learning about each other's cultures through direct contact with each other.

In Global Classrooms, two or more classrooms located anywhere in the world can study a common topic together, sharing what they are learning about a topic during a specified period of time. Global Classroom projects often address current issues and problems for which there are, as yet, no solutions. Classrooms can join together for gathering and analyzing data as well as discussing projects in progress.

Communicating with keypals is probably the most common telecomputing activity, similar in form to surface mail pen pal activities.

Newsgroups to Try

(To read these newsgroups, type **news:** into your Web browser's location indicator; followed by the name of the group—found in the left column.)

alt.good.morning	some interesting upbeat connections among the members	**rec.puzzles**	need a little brain-strain?
clari.news.briefs	regular news updates	**rec.scouting**	troop leaders and other interested adults voice their opinions and offer insights
clari.news.goodnews	something uplifting when the world seems completely crazy	**rec.baseball**	curve balls, basket catches, peanuts, and Cracker Jacks
clari.local.state name	just fill in your state's name and get briefs from that area	**rec.basketball**	slam-dunks, playoffs, MVPs, and contract hassles.
rec.arts.startrek.current	all about the latest iterations of the sci-fi classic	**rec.hockey**	from the land of the Stanley Cup, Zambonis, and missing teeth
rec.arts.movies	the world of cinema	**rec.travel**	bargains and tips for those on-the-road
rec.pets	dogs, cats, and the like	**misc.fitness**	news and tips on exercise
rec.sport.football.college	NCAA and NAIA football	**misc.education**	good overview of schooling, students, and teachers
rec.food.recipes	need an injection of creativity in the kitchen?	**misc.kids**	kids and their behavior
rec.food.cooking	more of the how-to than the above list	**misc.kids.computer**	software, hardware discussions for kids and parents alike
rec.backcountry	get out of the city with help from this group	**misc.jobs.offered**	looking for a new position?
rec.crafts.textiles	needlepoint, quilting, knitting, etc.	**misc.invest**	hints and tips on where to put your money
rec.games.misc	overall look at games of all types	**misc.writing**	discourse on issues and genres of writing
rec.games.video	narrowing the focus of games		
rec.gardens	lilies drooping when they should be the talk of the block?		

22

Reprinted from TCM 621 Internet for Kids, *Teacher Created Materials, 1996*

20

A Word Day

Get a new word, definition, and sample usage along with a cute quote each day. This can be an excellent start-of-the-day activity in your classroom.

http://www.wordsmith.org/awad/

Weather Watch

Students exchange, compare, and graph weather information with other students across the country and around the world.

Letter to the President

Ask your students to draft letters to the president of the United States. As you remind them to dot their i's and cross their t's, discuss how to write a persuasive letter. Mail their masterpieces to *president@whitehouse.gov*. They will get a response from an automated e-mail answering machine or occasionally a real person.

The Price Is Right

Students conduct surveys, collecting and comparing food, gas, or clothing prices from around the world.

Round-Robin Stories

Students in participating classes start a story. Each story starter is sent to a predetermined class, and the students add a new section to the story. Stories continue to rotate to the different classes until each story reaches the original class. Graphics can be added to illustrate the stories or create a book.

Plant Growing Contest

Students from a variety of geographical areas throughout the world plant the same kind of seeds on the same day, follow the same directions for the care of the plants as they grow, measure the plants, and send data to other participants so they can use these data for graphing, analyses, and drawing conclusions.

GeoGame

Each class sends local information such as the latitude, weather, natural resources, etc., to a facilitator. The facilitator sends the information to all participating classes, and they must determine the class locations based on the data provided.

Folk Tales to Tell

Exchange and collect regional, ethnic, and urban folk tales from various parts of the world (or country). Compare common themes

Students from a variety of geographical areas throughout the world plant the same kind of seeds on the same day, follow the same directions for the care of the plants as they grow, measure the plants, and send data to other participants so they can use these data for graphing, analyses, and drawing conclusions.

and discover what makes each story unique.

Shadows

Students throughout the world measure the lengths of shadows cast at the same time on the same date. Comparisons among latitude, shadow length, and time of year can be analyzed. Measures must be standardized (using metrics).

Pollution Patrol

Students measure the quality of the air and water (in lakes, oceans, or rain) and compare findings with students in other parts of the world. The impact of pollution and environmental factors can be addressed.

Postcard Exchange

Students from various parts of the world exchange picture postcards. Each class then connects the postcards to a large map as they arrive. Another idea is to have the students plan a fictional trip to visit their keypals, analyzing the best routes and modes of transportation, amount of money needed, and sites to see when they arrive.

Language Learning

Search on the Internet and locate newspapers, articles, or Web pages written in a foreign language for your students to translate.

TV Time

Contact students in other states and countries to survey their favorite television shows and movies. Students can investigate such issues as the following: "Students in which countries (or states) watch the most television? Which countries produce their own TV programs, and which ones dub their language on imported programs? How do the commercials differ from country to country?" These activities could lead into math graphing and statistics activities.

Culture Costs

In some countries, cultural performances, such as ballets, are subsidized by the government. Conduct surveys to find out how much a concert would cost in proportion to an average daily salary. Is a professional ballet more expensive or less expensive than a movie? Are the museums free for the public, or is there a fee?

Involve a Relative

If you or any of your students have a friend or relative who lives in a far-off land and would be willing to answer online questions about their home, students could develop a set of well-thought-out questions for them to answer, a great way to develop letter writing skills.

Contact students in other states and countries to survey their favorite television shows and movies.

Conduct an Online Survey

A common project for students is to conduct some type of survey and then tabulate and analyze the results. By using the Internet, the students will most likely receive responses from all over North America and the world. This type of project lends itself to all sorts of extension exercises: plotting the origin of respondents on a map, analyzing replies by various characteristics, etc. The best way to begin such a project is to plan it out with your students first. It is important to pick a survey topic that would make sense worldwide, not just in your state. Once the survey has been carefully considered, it can be posted on several education-related newsgroups and listservs. Make sure the intent is clear and that people can respond to an e-mail address. Survey topics might include school nutrition; attitudes about the use of computers in schools; voter registration; community history; favorite clothes, foods, school subjects, famous persons, and so on; best Internet sites; etc.

Monitor a Newsgroup

Is there a particular Internet newsgroup covering your current thematic unit topic? Find out and as a class, take part in it for a few weeks. Submit a question or, depending on the expertise of your students on the topic, answer a few. Caution: While newsgroups can be an extremely valuable source of information, there are a number of inappropriate newsgroups. The teacher should check out a particular newsgroup first, before using it with students.

Worldwide Shopping Basket

Have students come up with a list of 10 common foods they like and create a short e-mail survey designed to be used to compare prices. Send the survey via electronic e-mail to a teacher you know on the Internet and ask students to price each item and return the results via e-mail. Next, they can pass it on to at least four other people. Ask each of those four people to e-mail the survey back to you for tabulation. With a little luck you will soon have data for an interesting activity where you can discuss economics and the usefulness of the Internet for gathering information quickly. Just be sure to put a limit on the number of participants because this electronic "chain letter" can quickly get out of control!

Political E-Mail Letter

A common writing project is to compose and send a letter to a government or business official. Try it online. Connect to a local or regional government site; most list the e-mail addresses for public officials. The addresses are often printed in newsletters and brochures put out by government offices.

> A common writing project is to compose and send a letter to a government or business official.

OnlineClass: A Hassle-Free Approach

Are you looking to take part in an online project but are a little concerned about setting up and maintaining it? OnlineClass is an organization specializing in developing and maintaining online projects for K–12 schools. Project materials and activities are delivered via e-mail, classrooms take part in discussions with experts, and all projects are carefully monitored by OnlineClass staff at a reasonable cost. The e-mail address is *tbt@onlineclass.com*.

Collaboration with Another Classroom

There are many projects and sites online devoted to classroom collaborations. Rather than finding one of the heavily traveled sites, consider setting up your own. It could be with a school across town, in a rural area (if you live in the city), in a city (if you live in the country), or, possibly, the other side of the state or country. Instead of getting online to start it up, make a few telephone calls to the communities and the schools you want to target. Or try the Web66's International Registry of Schools:

http://web66.coled.umn.edu/schools.html

Guess Where?

Create a geographic scavenger hunt. Have your students prepare a list of geographic features and prominent landmarks in your area and challenge other schools across the Internet to identify the location of your school. If students get stumped, have them visit one of the many geographic servers on the Internet for help.

Virtual Biographies

Have students contact their keypals and exchange information about each other via e-mail. Developing a list of interview questions can help get this process going. Then ask students to write biographies of their keypals, called "An Imaginary Day in the Life of ___." The biographies could include what school is like, what happens before and after school, what responsibilities the keypals have, what their families are like, what they hope to be doing in five years, what they've done that they're proud of, and what they think of their schools and teachers. Keypals review the bios, pointing out the strengths, incorrect information and assumptions, and anything they don't want included. The bios are rewritten and returned. Students next read the biographies of themselves aloud to their classmates. The final step is to ask students to reflect orally and in writing on what they have learned from this experience.

> There are many projects and sites online devoted to classroom collaborations.

Impersonate a Literary Character

Collaborate ahead of time with keypal teachers to select a character-rich short story or novel that both classes are reading. Have students choose a character from the piece and recreate an event, telling it from the character's point of view and keeping the character's name secret so the keypal must guess who it is.

Adopt a Grandparent

Students and teachers might sometimes think they are the only ones using e-mail, but some senior citizens are online too. Some seniors enjoy corresponding with young people on just about any topic. In fact, nearly any subject a student discusses with another student via e-mail can just as easily be discussed with a senior citizen. One of the great things about seniors is that their perspectives can be quite different in comparison to those of students' peers.

Collaborate ahead of time with keypal teachers to select a character-rich short story or novel that both classes are reading.

KEYPALS

LET ME INTRODUCE MYSELF

Name: _____ Date:_____

Directions: Fill in the following information. It will help you write your introduction letter to your keypal.

About Me

Age:_____ Height: _____ Hair color: _____ Eye color: _____

Birthday: _____

My favorite things: _____

_____

What I like to do:_____

_____

My favorite subject in school: _____

_____

About My Family

Parents' names: _____

Sisters' and brothers' names: _____

Things we do together: _____

Places we like to go: _____

Our house: _____

Our pets:_____

About My School

School name: _____

Mascot: _____

Teacher's name(s): _____

Our day: _____

My favorite thing about school: _____

Other Things About Me

Reprinted from TCM 668 Internet for Teachers & Parents, *Teacher Created Materials,* 1996.

Name:

Virtual Tourist

URL:

http://www.vtourist.com

Description of Site:

The Virtual Tourist is an electronic map of the world, with each section consisting of a hypermedia link of general information and thousands of pictures of places all over the world.

What to Do There:

Use the media collected from this site to make pamphlets advertising places all over the world. Play an online geography scavenger hunt. Have students collect pictures and text about different countries that you assign. E-mail tourist information offices in different countries requesting information.

Reprinted from TCM 668 Internet for Teachers & Parents, *Teacher Created Materials,* 1996.

Adventure Online

Name:

Adventure Online

URL:

http://adventureonline.com/index.html

Description of Site:

Adventure Online is dedicated to bringing adventure and learning to K–12 classrooms and Internet explorers. Serving as a guide to adventure related projects, Adventure Online features exclusive expeditions, adventure news, and entertaining games, as well as developing educational expeditions and adventures. Adventure Online also highlights other projects of educational significance.

What to Do There:

Students can take part virtually in several adventures with explorers from around the world. The geography scavenger hunt game, which features unnamed photos from different parts of the world, is particularly good. Weekly clues are given to evoke the sleuth in all of us. Participants must e-mail their responses, and winners are awarded wonderful gifts.

Reprinted from TCM 668 Internet for Teachers & Parents, *Teacher Created Materials,* 1996.

E-Mail Etiquette

There is an etiquette associated with e-mail, as there is with all Internet tools. Most of it has to do with recognizing that there are many kinds of computers operating many kinds of mail readers, all with different sets of features.

- Use plain text.
- Be extremely careful with humor. E-mail tends to be much less formal than traditional paper mail. Even so, care needs to be taken when sending e-mail to people you don't know well; subtle wit travels poorly in e-mail. If you use wit that might be mistaken as attack or criticism, you can clarify your intent with a "smiley." A smiley is a set of text characters that forms a face when you look at it sideways. People use smileys on the Internet to signify their real emotional intent. A common smiley is : -) which denotes a happy or light mood.
- Don't send anything through electronic mail that you wouldn't write on the chalkboard in your classroom. A good rule of thumb is to assume that any message you send via the Internet is potentially readable by someone other than the intended recipient. For that reason, don't send any credit card information or Social Security numbers over the Internet.
- Flaming is the term used for inflammatory messages on the Internet. Basically, no matter how angry you or your students feel about what some other Internet surfer says, resist the temptation to respond angrily to him or her. Instead, use that energy to do something else.
- Don't type in all capital letters. Capital letters leap off the screen and can be really annoying. It is the equivalent to screaming!
- Talk to your students about what is appropriate to send through e-mail. There are some things that you don't want to discuss via e-mail because they are too personal in nature or are best said in writing (the old-fashioned way) or in person. Brainstorm with your students a list of appropriate and inappropriate uses of electronic mail.

There is an etiquette associated with e-mail, as there is with all Internet tools.

FTP and Telnet

FTP (File Transfer Protocol)

FTP is an extremely useful tool for educators and students. With the FTP program on the Internet, files and computer software can be obtained and downloaded into the user's computer. For instance, if students in New Zealand wanted to get the book *Alice in Wonderland* from the library at the University of Maryland, they would simply open up the FTP option, find the University of Maryland, choose the children's section of the library, and then find the book. The text of the book would appear through the Internet and could then be downloaded into the student's own files. A problem occasionally occurs when FTP is used to download a file. Sometimes a file or piece of software contains a computer virus. It is, therefore, necessary to scan all files accessed through FTP before they are used.

Telnet

Telnet is another extremely useful Internet tool for educators and teachers. Through Telnet, remote access is possible from other computer sites. Through Telnet, it is possible for the teacher to access and log on to their school computer from any other computer that is connected to the Internet anywhere in the world! Files can be downloaded, e-mail messages can be checked, and any other feature can be accomplished that would normally be done on an office computer. Students can use the same technique to alter computer assignments they have been working on. A user just opens the Telnet application, then types his or her server's name, account, and password, and Telnet opens the account just as if the user were at his or her original work or school computer.

World Wide Web

The World Wide Web makes up a very large percent of the Internet. Nearly seventy percent of all information searches are handled through the World Wide Web, and this is where most educators and students find their information on nearly any subject. The Web is only part of the Internet. Information is found quickly in the World Wide Web through typing in keywords or filenames. The World Wide Web has thousands of interesting sites such as the president's Web site and NASA's Space Center.

Some of the most creative uses of the Internet can start by using the World Wide Web as a search tool for information on assignments or projects. Through the World Wide Web, students can create their own home page, they can create a student or school magazine, or they can simply use it to find other sources of current information.

In reality, the uses of the World Wide Web are only limited by the imagination or creativity of the user. The information necessary to learn just about anything is probably contained somewhere on the Web; it is just up to the user to find it and learn from it.

Nearly seventy percent of all information searches are handled through the World Wide Web, and this is where most educators and students find their information on nearly any subject.

Elementary Problem of the Week

Name:

Elementary Problem of the Week

URL:

http://forum.swarthmore.edu/sum95/ruth/elem.pow.html

Description of Site:

High school students pose challenging problems for elementary students each week.

What to Do There:

This is one of hundreds of grass-roots mathematics projects out there that will help you bring spice to your math program. Log on each week and print out the problem of the week. After your students have solved the problem, post the answer in their posting section. They will be rewarded for attempting whether they are right or not.

Reprinted from TCM 668 Internet for Teachers & Parents, *Teacher Created Materials,* 1996.

Name:

Ask Dr. Math

URL:

http://forum.swarthmore.edu/dr.math/

Description of Site:

This site is the place to go when you want answers. If you or your students have questions about a math problem, Dr. Math will help you figure it out.

What to Do There:

Submit your K–12 math question by sending e-mail to dr.math@forum.swarthmore.edu. Tell them what you know about your problem and where you are stuck. Dr. Math will reply to you via e-mail.

Reprinted from TCM 668 Internet for Teachers & Parents, *Teacher Created Materials,* 1996.

Implementation

"The Net is like a huge vandalized library. Someone has destroyed the catalog and removed the front matter, indexes, etc., from hundreds of thousands of books and torn and scattered what remains. "Surfing" is the process of sifting through this disorganized mess in the hope of coming across some useful fragments of text and images that can be related to other fragments. The Net is even worse than a vandalized library because thousands of additional unorganized fragments are added daily by the myriad cranks, sages, and persons with time on their hands who launch their unfiltered messages into cyberspace" (Gorman, p. 34).

Searching

It is relatively easy to access a Web site when the address is known, but with millions of Web sites available, how do you find sites when you do not know the precise addresses?

Since there are millions of computers connected to the Internet, no one can list all of the sites around the world. Each computer is like an independent library putting more up-to-the-minute information at the fingertips of educators and students. Because these "libraries"

It is relatively easy to access a Web site when the address is known, but with millions of Web sites available, how do you find sites when you do not know the precise address?

each have their own organizational system, finding information on a given topic is like trying to find the proverbial needle in a haystack. Finding information about a certain topic can really be a challenge because a new Web site is being added to the Internet every four seconds! Thankfully, there are online tools which can help you search the Internet to find just the information you need.

A search engine is one such online tool. A search engine is a program that searches a database of Web documents for words you supply and then lists the hyperlinks to sites that contain those words. You can use one of the Web's many search engines to locate specific information requested.

Another online tool to help you find information is the search directory.

Search engines generally present forms for you to fill out. In the simplest engines, you click in the entry field and type one or more keywords identifying what you are looking for. When you press the "enter" or "return" key, the searching begins. Some search engines include various options that narrow the search and often result in a more meaningful list of links.

Examples of popular search engines include the following:

AltaVista	*http://www.altavista.com*
Infoseek	*http://www.infoseek.go.com/*
Lycos	*http://www.lycos.com*
HotBot	*http://www.hotbot.com*
Excite	*http://www.excite.com*
Yahoo!	*http://www.yahoo.com*

Another online tool to help you find information is the search directory. The search directory is a tool that provides general listings of topics. You should use a search directory when you are looking for a general topic or category, such as geography, wars, dogs, baseball, television, etc. If you want to find a Web site on a specific topic or answer a question, then use a search engine.

One popular search directory is Yahoo! The Yahoo! site (*http: www.yahoo.com*) contains a search tree.

Yahoo! lists categories that can be used to find Web sites. Yahoo! is a hierarchical index to the World Wide Web. You can browse such categories as art, education, government, reference, and social science, refining your search until you find pages that interest you. Yahoo! has a couple of dozen major categories and many hundreds of subcategories.

Clicking on a category produces a large list of subcategories. As you continue making selections, the list is narrowed until Yahoo! finally displays a list of appropriate sites, including descriptions

A Look At Search Engines

Once you are on the Web, try out a variety of the many search tools offered. You will likely find one that will become a favorite, for awhile at least. (You may want to consider changing about once a month, for reasons such as speed and the relevance of hits [the references that the search tool returns].)

For most of us, simply typing in one or more words into the one-line text field and clicking the search button will get us most of what we need. But for those instances where that is not the case, here are a few search tips that will help you track down that desired data or Web site.

1. Start your search in your mind at first. Try to narrow your subject enough so the search engine can return reasonably relevant hits. For example, for information on Willie Mays, enter his name rather than San Francisco Giants.

2. Unless capitalization matters, stick with lowercase characters.

3. Punctuation is usually ignored, so Willie Mays is the same as Mays, Willie and Mays Willie.

4. Consider bookmarking a page of your search engine's results for quicker return to information you might need a day or two later.

5. Explore the advanced options that most search tools offer you.

52

Reprinted from TCM 621 Internet for Kids, *Teacher Created Materials, 1996*

35

and links to the sites. Remember, however, the search tree has determined which sites to include; the list is not all inclusive. Sometimes the sites are rated by an organization that has produced the search tree, based on what they believe the usefulness of the site to be. The ratings are sometimes in the form of stars: four stars for very useful to one star for somewhat useful.

Sometimes, search engines and search directories return many more hyperlinks than it is possible to access. For example, the search criterion CHINA found more than 19,000 matches. Many of the matches were for Chinese restaurants located all over the world or for museums containing Chinese artifacts. Therefore, refer to the list of searching tips below.

Another popular
search director, aimed
specifically for
students, is
Yahooligans!

Another popular search director, aimed specifically for students, is Yahooligans! (*http://www.yahooligans.com*). Sites in this directory are usually considered safe for students under 15 years of age.

Searching Tips

- Read the directions. Although this sounds obvious, many of the online search tools come with instructions or a help area. They can be very useful.

- Try different search tools. For each search engine or directory you try, you will get different results. Each tool searches the Internet in a slightly different way. They use different databases, so they will locate different Web sites for you. Also, their databases change constantly, so a search on one day may not find the exact same Web sites on another day.

- Use keywords. Rather than long phrases, try to use main words that sum up your desired topic.

- Watch your spelling. For a computer to make a successful search, you must give it proper instructions.

- For proper names or phrases, use quotation marks to link words together in the search.

- To make your search as accurate as possible, use the terms *and* or *not* (Boolean logic). If you enter *women + history*, you will get sites that will have both the words "women" and "history," while "women" or "history" will return sites that contain either the word "women" or the word "history."

History or GO List

As you move from site to site on the Internet, it is helpful to be able to return to a previously visited site. One method is to continue clicking on the "back" button until the site is reached. A more efficient method would be to access the history list, which is a list of the sites you have been to. Displaying the "go" menu displays the history list. Selecting an address from that menu will access that site.

Bookmarks

The history list works well for sites visited during a single session, but how can you return to sites days or weeks after visiting them? A Web bookmark is a Web page address that you type once and save under a familiar name. A bookmark stores in a file the name and address of a selected site so that it can be accessed at a later time. To add a bookmark for the currently displayed Web page, select the "Add Bookmark" (for *Netscape Navigator*) or "Add Favorites" (for *Internet Explorer*) command from the menu. The name of the bookmarked site is added to the bookmark menu. To later access a bookmarked site, select its name from the bottom of the bookmark's menu.

Sometimes connecting to a Web site may take longer than you expect. The problem is not with your software, although several factors may affect connection time, including how fast your modem is and how far away the site is. One of the most important factors, however, is the server that you are contacting. Some extremely popular servers may be processing many requests for use at the same time, and some servers are just slower than others.

To add a bookmark for the currently displayed Web page, select the "Add Bookmark" (for *Netscape Navigator*) or "Add Favorites" (for *Internet Explorer*) command from the menu.

Evaluating Sources

Just as you become aware of how difficult it might be to find the information you want on the Web unless you know the appropriate address, there is another consideration. There is the problem of finding useful and accurate information.

Some Web authors do not give a lot of thought to how the information at their sites will be retrieved. Many Web documents lack titles that clearly describe the documents or introductions that can be used to determine whether the documents are appropriate for use by you or your students.

In researching a project on the Internet, it is important to evaluate the source of the information you will use. Remember, anyone can post information on the Internet. There are no rules as to accuracy or reliability of the information. This means that you must discriminate, read carefully, and check your sources. More importantly, you must teach your students how to be discerning Internet users. Just because it is on the Internet doesn't mean it's true.

After the search, you and your students should ask some questions:

- What does the article or information say? Does it answer the question you asked at the beginning of the search?
- What is the primary source of the information? You may be more likely to trust information posted by NASA than information posted by a high school student who cites no sources.
- Who is the author? Who else is mentioned in the information? Does the author post credentials?
- Is the information factual or the opinion of the author? What is the author's viewpoint? Do you agree or disagree?
- When was the information written? Is it current enough to use? On what date was the publication posted?
- How can you check the information with another source? (either online or perhaps in the media center)

Searching Tips for Educators

The Internet is often referred to as an ocean because of its enormity and power. Some people are said to surf the Net. It is probably more accurate to say that most people swim through the Internet until they start finding their way.

Hotlist

One of the first steps in using the Internet's power in the classroom is linking to Web sites that you will find useful for your students.

One of the first steps in using the Internet's power in the classroom is linking to Web sites that you will find useful for your students. This can be done through bookmarks, but it is a much more efficient process to create a Web page that collects locations in a hotlist. This will save your learners hours of aimless surfing. You can share (or swap) this hotlist with colleagues across the hall (or across the hemisphere!).

Treasure Hunt

When it is time for learners to develop content knowledge, create a treasure hunt (or scavenger hunt) for them. Here you will pose questions about the topic and provide interesting Web resources that hold the answers. A smartly designed treasure hunt can go far beyond finding unrelated nuggets of knowledge. By choosing questions that define the scope or parameters of the topic, you lead the students to discover that through their answers they are tapping into a deeper vein of thought. Finally, by including a culminating question, you give students the opportunity to synthesize what they have learned and shape it into a broader understanding of the big picture.

Sampler: In a subject sampler learners are presented with a small variety of intriguing Web sites organized around a main topic. What makes this a particularly effective way to engage student involvement is that first off, the Web sites themselves offer something interesting to do, read, or see. Learners are asked to respond to the Web-based activities from a personal perspective. Rather than uncovering hard knowledge (as in a scavenger hunt), students are asked about their perspectives on topics and to make comparisons to experiences they have had and to give their interpretations of artworks or data, etc. The use of a student sampler is important when you want your students to feel connected to a topic and to feel that the subject really matters.

WebQuest: When it is time to go beyond facts and feelings, to get into more challenging aspects of a topic (which tend to require knowledge and to engage feelings), learners may be ready to tackle a WebQuest. Basically, this strategy presents student groups with a challenging task or scenario or a problem to solve. Students are then provided with all the resources they need to explore and make sense of the issues involved in the challenge. Typically, the students conclude by synthesizing their learning in a summarizing act. A WebQuest is a great activity to quickly immerse students in real learning. (See the chapter on WebQuests.)

> **It is important to remember that the primary purpose of a citation is to allow the reader to locate the cited information.**

Citing Web Sources

It is important to remember that the primary purpose of a citation is to allow the reader to locate the cited information. That is especially true when citing Web sources. As of yet, the academic world has not agreed to a single citation standard, but one of the more widely accepted forms is that published by the Modern Language Association in its publication *MLA Handbook.* Several Web sites also have examples of citations for material found on the Internet. Most of these sites are similar to the MLA guidelines with the addition of the URL where the information was found. The general form of a citation is

> Author's Last Name, First Name MI. "Title of Document." *Title of Journal, Newsletter* or *something similar.* Volume number (year of publication: number of pages or paragraphs). Online. Internet. Available http: URL

or

> Author. Title of Item. (Online) Available *http://address/filename,* date of document or download.

In many cases the name of the author will not be provided. In this case, corporate authorship may be used, but be careful to make clear what organization has produced the cited text. Often the institution running the server containing the text cannot be assumed to be the sponsor. If the source is an article with a date of publication, use that date; otherwise, use the date the text was accessed. This is important because resources found on the Web can change frequently.

Critical reading of resources has always been an important educational objective. Now with the arrival of millions of resources via the Internet, students' abilities to evaluate their credibility is increasingly important.

Copyright and Fair Use

When using the Internet, it is the user's responsibility to understand the rules. Educators have an obligation not only to respect copyright laws but also to teach their students what copyright means and why it is important to them. Do not allow your students to believe the myth, "If it is on the Net and there is no copyright symbol, anyone can use it." According to the Berne Convention for the Protection of Literary and Artistic Works, almost all "writings" produced in the United States after April 1, 1989, are automatically copyrighted and protected regardless of whether a copyright symbol is present.

The laws on fair use and copyright are very vague. The concept of fair use is the means by which educators of nonprofit educational institutions may use copyrighted materials without seeking permission or making payment to the author or publisher. This is a controversial idea.

It is the ease with which educators and students can incorporate copyrighted works of others that makes this relatively new and powerful educational tool a perplexing issue for everyone. In 1996 a set of guidelines called "Fair Use Guidelines for Educational Multimedia" was developed. Even it is subject to interpretation. As technologies evolve and change, the boundaries of fair use will always be unclear. It is important to keep in mind the purpose of the copyright law. The purpose is to prevent financial harm to persons or companies involved in creating intellectual property.

A good rule of thumb for educators is to have students use public domain resources for their projects or to get written permission for materials they intend to use from the Web. While it is permissible for students to incorporate copyrighted music or graphics in their multimedia projects, it is not permissible to distribute these projects over the Web outside of the school. For projects to be distributed outside of a school setting, such as the WWW, they need to be made with original or public domain content or have permission from the persons who hold copyrights to parts of the content.

Student Plagiarism

The emergence of Internet sites for the purpose of essay exchange has led to what some students might see as an easy way out of doing their schoolwork. A good site for educators to consider if faced with this issue is *http://www.carleton.ca/~gsenecha/guide/*. It is the *Instructor's Guide to Internet Plagiarism.* The purpose of the site is to help educators determine if a given piece of academic work has been obtained from the Internet.

> *"'Tis true: there's magic in the web of it."*
>
> William Shakespeare
> *Othello*—Act 3, Scene 4

The emergence of Internet sites for the purpose of essay exchange has led to what some students might see as an easy way out of doing their schoolwork.

Curriculum Resources

Reference materials
provide one of the
main supplements to
an educator's
instructional program.

A wide variety of information is afforded students and teachers who have access to the Internet. Predominantly, the content of the Net is information and opinion; what tends to be in shorter supply are the specific learning activities that make use of this wealth. The Internet may be an embarrassment of riches that is next to worthless without an educator to facilitate learning and integration in classrooms.

References

Reference materials provide one of the main supplements to an educator's instructional program. Textbooks, encyclopedias, and media collections are definitive references that may be searched, studied, or browsed in order to supply additional information. Similarly, Web sites exist that can provide the same kind of support for teachers and students. Web-based references are the first main informational types of sites that educators will find useful. References can be in the form of databases that collect a wide body of information, like the *CIA World Fact Book* and *The Statistical Abstract of the United States,* while regular online use of the *HyperText Dictionary* is likely to sharpen anyone's vocabulary.

Another way to use references is to go directly to sites that catalog other Web sites into hierarchical lists. Such locations as the WWW Virtual Library or Yahoo! are good places to start if you are curious about a range of topics and do not want to limit your investigation to the keywords needed by search engines. Browsing through the headings will give you an idea whether enough references exist on a topic to make it worth pursuing. Although no free commercial encyclopedia exists on the Web, several publishers provide samples from their extensive databases. Actual encyclopedias, such as the *Encyclopedia Britannica,* are also commercially available online if you choose to subscribe. *Encyclopedia Britannica* has a wonderful collection of biographies and pictures of Olympic athletes, a calendar of people in history, and a gallery of other materials. *Grolier Online* has an excellent presentation titled "The American Presidency." Microsoft's *Encarta Schoolhouse* provides information on specific topics while pointing to other *Encarta* articles and Web links. Themes currently available are the American Civil War, environment, and earthquakes.

You can easily search hypertext versions of a rhyming dictionary, *Webster's Dictionary* or *Roget's Thesaurus.* Phrases, passages, and proverbs can be viewed at *Project Bartleby,* which is based on the 1901 edition of *Bartlett's Familiar Quotations.* Even though the thesaurus and quotations are dated, they can still be useful as part of an online reference collection.

To study a foreign language, get ready for a trip abroad, or study a culture of a country, visit the Online Language Dictionaries and Translators Web site, a link of lexicon lists and dictionaries from Afrikaans to Zulu.

Each year the U. S. Labor Department publishes the *Occupational Outlook Handbook,* a valuable tool for media specialists, vocational instructors, and counselors who assist students with career decisions.

Celebrations are enjoyed by all. With so many special days, weeks, anniversaries, and holidays, the best place to start is by browsing Yahoo!'s Society and Cultures: Holidays page. It is a virtual passageway to hundreds of interesting religious and secular events.

Access to current information about governments and their leaders is critical in our changing world.

Access to current information about governments and their leaders is critical in our changing world. Web Central Government Resources answers a wealth of reference inquiries with links to government agencies, foreign embassies, the *CIA World Factbook,* Rulers of the World, and the United Nations Headquarters. Students asking for pictures of foreign flags can find them at Flags of All Countries.

The Electronic Zoo, Endangered Species, and VetPedia should answer questions about animals and their well-being. Students inquisitive about space can explore the Nine Planets or see the earth in an entirely different way through the Earth Viewer. Chemistry students can retrieve technical data on the first 112 elements, using the interactive WebElement site.

Educators will most likely find several key references in an area of interest and then become comfortable with what is available. The vastness of the Internet guarantees exhaustion if you think you must find every last piece of information on a topic. Instead, by finding references appropriate to interests, degree of expertise, and grade level, educators can tap into support material that could not be obtained this easily anywhere else.

> The vastness of the Internet guarantees exhaustion if you think you must find every last piece of information on a topic.

Online Tutorials

Generally, an online tutorial or lesson targets specific learner outcomes and guides a user through instructional steps, often with feedback or checkpoints. Classic examples are the frog dissection sites. The Interactive Frog Dissection is a guided tutorial with feedback, video, and scanned images. The Virtual Frog Dissection Kit provides excellent computer-generated graphics. Such detailed Web sites are great application sites for teachers. However, not enough of these types of sites currently exist on the Web.

Online Science Fairs

Science projects allow students using the scientific method to define, investigate, and synthesize their own concepts.

CyberFair

A Minnesota school site written for and by students in grades three through six allows students to see a sampling of elementary projects. In addition, there are two concise, expertly written guides: "Experimental Science Projects" by David Morano, Associate Professor, Mankato State University, and "Steps to Prepare a Science Fair Project" by Yvonne Karsten can be very useful in your classroom. Karsten's suggestions on what makes a good science project, her ideas list, and paper guidelines will be especially helpful to students.

Explorer

Jointly developed by the Great Lakes Collaborative and the University of Kansas UNITE Group, Explorer is a collection of lab activities and lesson plans for K–12 teachers. Many lessons can be used to teach scientific methods of observation and analysis. Particularly beneficial are the activities on statistics and probability in the mathematical folder. Each activity was written by an educator and is labeled with the appropriate grade.

Science Project Handbook

A model handbook to assist students with the science fair process is an example from the Collier County Schools, Florida. It is well organized and loaded with information from the reasons to do a science project to expectations, time line, glossary, categories, choosing a topic, data checklists, the display, and judging criteria.

New Jersey NIE Project: As a Science/Math Expert

At no other time in history has there been this kind of direct access to the scientific community. Thanks to the many scientists who have volunteered their time and energy to support young minds, students in grades K–12 can ask questions and receive responses via e-mail in a timely fashion. This New Jersey site is a pipeline to these professionals.

> At no other time in history has there been this kind of direct access to the scientific community.

Science Learning Network

Whimsical artwork accompanies a multitude of elementary hands-on activities at the Thinking Fountain. Students can create their own tools for investigation and then use them to conduct experiments. For example, they can make an acid-base indicator strip, using paper towels and a concoction of red cabbage. They can then test different liquids and observe the results. Complete step-by-step instructions are provided.

StemNet Science Fair Home Page

StemNet provides a comprehensive list of science fair projects organized by grade level from primary through high school. Suggestions for the lower grades are geared toward demonstrations and models while ideas for the upper grades focus on experimentation and sophisticated investigation.

The T.W.I.N.K.I.E.S. Project

Humor is used to describe procedures, observations, and possible applications when experimenting with the cream-filled sponge cake. Nuke them in the microwave to find out just how resistant they are to radiation. Dunk them in water to see their solubility. Blend them to see how much air they contain.

Access Excellence

One of the richest sources of biology and biotechnology material is on this Web site. You can actively discuss a variety of subjects through online seminars, join a teachers' discussion group, read the latest news about science discoveries, or browse the hundreds of classroom activities written by teachers.

Cornell Theory Center Math and Science Gateway

Teachers and students in grades 9–12 will appreciate this site designed to meet their more advanced needs. There is information about astronomy, biology, chemistry, computing, the environment, health, mathematics, and physics.

Frank Potter's Science Gems

Nearly two thousand annotated locations are categorized by subject and grade level on this Web page. It is updated frequently and covers physical science, earth science, life science, mathematics, technology, engineering, and health.

There is information about astronomy, biology, chemistry, computing, the environment, health, mathematics, and physics.

NASA Spacelink

This page presents by subject a list of links by that can be used to locate a tremendous amount of research material.

Bill Nye, the Science Guy

This upbeat Web site, based on the popular PBS television show, is designed to interest children in the world of science. Discover fast facts and experiments from the pulldown menus in the guide.

Tellecollaborative Learning Around the World

Name:

Telecollaborative Learning Around the World

URL:

http://www.home.talkcity.com/academydr/nicknacks/

Description of Site:

NickNacks' primary goal is to encourage collaborations among educators and students around the world. Whether you want to participate in a lesson or start your own, there is information here to help you. Together we can build a better place to live, grow, and learn.

What to Do There:

Want to take part in collaborative lessons with classes all over the world? Here is a great place to start. If you don't find a project you like, make up your own. They will help you with starting your own project, as well as help you get other classes to participate.

Reprinted from TCM 668 Internet for Teachers & Parents, *Teacher Created Materials,* 1996.

Integrating the Internet

Name:

Integrating the Internet

URL:

http://www.indirect.com/www/dhixson/index.html

Description of Site:

Lots of people are talking about this topic, but there are relatively few places to go to find out about it. Look here to find primary resources, projects, a weekly newsletter, units of study, and a tutorial to help you plan projects and classroom home pages.

What to Do There:

This site has several activities in the science area. Ready to make the jump to producing your own pages on the Web? Susan Hixson has given you everything you need to do it here—from directions on design and producing, to how you get Web space, to placing your document.

Reprinted from TCM 668 Internet for Teachers & Parents, *Teacher Created Materials,* 1996.

Publishing Student Work Online

Web educational content consists mainly of information posted on the Web for students and teachers to read. It is generally excellent information and opens a whole new world of resources to the school environment. With such a wealth of expert information, what can be gained by having students post their own research and writings online?

The answer lies in the process of communication, not just in the result. Students are eager to publish online. Teachers report that whole classrooms will gather around the computer to see their work come up on the screen and that those who get chosen for Web publication become instant classroom heroes. Students express themselves better and more readily if they feel there is a sympathetic audience for their work. E-mail and Web publishing allow students to be heard and to be judged by both their peers and by the adults in their world.

The Web as a medium seems to offer something that traditional methods do not. It shows that we take students seriously and that we value what they say. It shows them that they have a chance to become contributors in a world of professional communicators. It allows them to present ideas with immediacy and a volume that has never before been available. For teachers, publication becomes both a reward for good work and a way of showing parents and the community what is going on in the classroom.

As students get better and better at handling the mechanics and the power of e-mail, they learn how language works, and they learn the power of their own voices. Research grows in depth. Opinions build in logic. Creative expression increases in volume as students see themselves in print and trust that they will be published and read.

With such a wealth of expert information, what can be gained by having students post their own research and writings online?

Resources

According to the HyperText Webster Dictionary, a "resource" is "a new or a reserve source of supply or support." Educationally, this usually refers to extra supporting experiences and materials like field trips, videotapes, guest speakers, libraries, and special interest magazines. These differ from references in their scope and depth; a reference attempts to be a complete collection that is often searchable. A resource makes no attempt at completeness but targets providing a deeper slice of additional information or experiences.

Resources abound on the Web. One type of resource is collections. Examples might include the Selected Civil War Photographs Homepage from the Library of Congress, Common Birds of the Australian National Botanic Gardens, CNN Interactive, Web 66 Registry of Schools Online or Pacific Bell Education First's Blue Web'n. Many of these types of Web sites perform the hotlisting function of searching, gathering, and collecting links to other sites on the Internet.

Besides a wealth of diverse collections, like the traditional classroom resource we call the field trip, the Web offers an array of online examples. Take virtual field trips to the Human Heart (from the Franklin Institute) or travel Around-the-World via Russell Gilbert's online journal.

To provide a more interactive virtual experience, you might want to get started with interactive videoconferencing. By using ISDN lines or Internet-based conferencing systems, such as Cornell University's CU-SeeMe, you can connect with real people and content providers from around the world. Look to The Liberty Science Center, The Museum of Television and Radio, and The San Diego Zoo to provide outstanding experiences for students. It could be that even more effective for student learning is reaching students from around the world to share ideas, information, and insights with peers.

Projects

Long-term projects have always held an important role in quality education. Research shows that students bring more cognitive tools to bear when they can turn their attention to a problem over a long period of time (Fisher, Dwyer, and Yocam, 1996). Teachers typically create longer units or projects around topics central to grade level requirements or frameworks. Often the projects involve interdisciplinary research, reading, writing, and artistic creations. Full-scale, long-term Web based projects start with the same premise but then add all the features and power of the Internet to create a real world, not classroom, context.

While a typical classroom might study the Mayans by using encyclopedias, *National Geographic* magazines, reference books, and maybe a video, students who have Internet access can participate in Mayaquest, a "wholly kid directed bicycle expedition into the Mayan world of Guatemala, Mexico, Belize, and Honduras." Students work to unravel the mystery behind the fall of the Mayan civilization. Through the process students have learned about ancient civilizations, math, science, geography, art, architecture, and the links between Maya and present-day civilizations. Satellite-linked computers allow cyclists and students anywhere in the United States to interact daily to

Long-term projects have always held an important role in quality education.

come to mutual decisions during the quest. The learning experience is unlike any ever before offered to students. World Wide Web resources and references, teaching guides, videoconferencing, e-mail, and offline endeavors combine to empower learners as contributing experts and/or data collectors who explore particular components of the project's focus.

Activities

Activities are the heart of what goes on in the classroom. A teacher may begin with a challenging invitation, engage students in a discussion, focus on defining key terms or concepts, and then set the students off on a group discovery, using reference materials, textbooks, and computers. Many different types of educational strategies are involved, and many different types of information are available to be processed. This type of orchestrating of learning experiences into a purposeful whole is what good teachers do all the time.

Although hands-on, problem-solving activities are the heart of an engaged classroom, they are, unfortunately, in short supply on the World Wide Web. Class activities tend to integrate and pull from many references and resources so that students can construct meaning from multiple inputs. Creating activities is a main strategy for classroom teachers to use to integrate the Web into their students' learning.

Because most often people view learning as acquiring new information, a site to check out might be the Black History Past to Present, a treasure hunt in which students are asked questions and are provided a matching list of Web sites they must explore to discover the answers. One specific outcome-oriented learning activity is known as the WebQuest. As a reminder, a WebQuest is a Web page that challenges a group of students with an authentic learning task and a rich set of Web resources, references, tools, and lessons linked directly to the page. (See the chapter on WebQuests.)

Teachers should take pride in the research findings that show that how an instructor embeds or frames an activity contributes more to its success than the activity itself standing alone. So even the best Web-based activity is going to need the context that you provide.

With the World Wide Web and all the accompanying features of the Internet, teachers have tools that will promote the best in cognitive and affective learning, expand the role of teachers to reflect the mentorship that Socrates modeled, and remove the walls that keep us in isolation.

Activities are the heart of what goes on in the classroom.

School District Web Sites: What Works?

What makes a good Web site? One quality is timeliness. People don't read the same news magazine over and over again, and they don't go back to the same stale Web pages.

A Web site needs to be treated as a publication; it needs to be dynamic, and it needs to be interesting. A good example of a school district Web site is in Birdville, Texas. Internet visitors can click on Birdville's home page and find synopses of recent school board actions and agendas for upcoming meetings. There are news releases on student awards and new-student preregistration, e-mail listings for all seven board members, and links to other sites from the Texas Department of Education to the White House.

A good site is also interactive—it allows the public to communicate with the district, says Maureen Reusche, Director of Curriculum and Technology for the Radnor (PA) School District. And that means someone had better answer the mail. Another sign of a successful school district Web site is its ability to strengthen community ties.

A Web site needs to be treated as a publication; it needs to be dynamic, and it needs to be interesting.

Name:

Teacher Created Materials

URL:

http://www.teachercreated.com

Description of Site:

Teacher Created Materials, Inc., publishes teacher-made, tested, and approved materials (including this book). This site offers free lesson plans and other teacher resources. Check out the technology materials they offer.

What to Do There:

I know, a shameless plug for Teacher Created Materials, but the materials are the best on the market because teachers like you create them. Send them an e-mail if you have materials that you would like published. Proposals should include an outline of the unit and two to three sample pages. You never know; you might be published and get paid for something that you already do in the classroom.

Reprinted from TCM 668 Internet for Teachers & Parents, *Teacher Created Materials,* 1996.

Name:

Global SchoolNet

URL:

http://www.gsn.org

Description of Site:

Global SchoolNet is a storehouse of hundreds of Internet resources for teachers.

What to Do There:

This award winning site is in the author's opinion one of the best the Web has to offer for teaching and learning. Check out the "Projects" link for information on several ongoing collaborative projects in which you can connect your students and classrooms with others all over the world. Create your own project or just join in on one that has already been developed. It is exciting, authentic learning and fun at the same time.

Reprinted from TCM 668 Internet for Teachers and Parents, *Teacher Created Materials,* 1996.

WebQuests

Definition

A WebQuest is defined by Bernie Dodge (San Diego State University), who coined the term, as "an inquiry-oriented activity in which some or all of the information that learners interact with comes from resources on the Internet." It is a great model for teachers searching for ways to incorporate the Internet into the classroom on both short-term and long-term bases.

In a short-term WebQuest, the teacher will locate and organize existing Web sites on a specific topic and design an interesting task around those sites. The end result will be a Web document that will engage students in pursuit of information and understanding for one or two class periods. The instructional goal of a short-term WebQuest is knowledge acquisition and integration. The learner deals with a significant amount of new information and makes sense of it.

Web-Based Interdisciplinary Unit

The long-term Web project is an interdisciplinary unit that will involve students for at least a week. At least two content areas will be involved and a major component of the unit will involve students looking for information on the Web. Non-Web and non-technology-based resources may also be involved as appropriate. The unit will be documented in enough detail so that another teacher could pick it up and implement it without ever meeting the author face to face. Included in a long-term WebQuest is an introduction overview for the teacher, lesson plans for individual classes, and any handouts or files needed by students. The instructional goal is extending and refining knowledge. The learner deeply analyzes a body of knowledge, transforms it, and demonstrates understanding by presenting it in some way; the unit is designed to take between a week and a month or more.

Components of a WebQuest

WebQuests are deliberately designed to make the best use of a learner's time. There is questionable educational benefit in having learners surfing the Net without a clear task in mind. To achieve that efficiency and clarity of purpose, WebQuests should contain at least the following components:

- An introduction should set the stage and provide brief background information necessary to understand the content and structure of the problem or challenge.

- The task is the problem posed to the learner for a solution, posed either to individuals or to groups. The task should be achievable and interesting.

- Information sources are needed to complete the task. Many of the resources are embedded in the WebQuest document itself as anchors pointing to information on the World Wide Web. The information sources might include Web documents, experts available via e-mail, searchable databases on the Net, books, and other documents physically available in the learner's setting. It might include a hyperlinked list of information sources and tools relevant to the topic.

- Process provides the learner with the means to make the best use of the resources. It includes a description of the clearly described steps the learners must go through to accomplish the task.

- Guidance is necessary to help the students organize the information acquired. It may be in the form of time lines, concept maps, diagrams, suggested action plans, tips for searching the Internet, options for organizing collected information, problem-solving techniques, and criteria for selection of Internet information.

- Conclusion will bring closure to the WebQuest, reminding the learners of what they have learned. The conclusion will be a product produced by the learner. It requires the learner to submit evidence of the WebQuest activity, such as a complete action plan, position paper or essay, presentation or recommendation report, self-created Web page, or some other relevant final project.

- A hypertext glossary would include a glossary of definitions of terms used or terms needed by the students to understand how to implement the project.
- Reflection/Assessment would include quality of participation, test of knowledge/solution of a problem, possibilities for further learning with a series of pointed questions, and the overall learning value of the project.

Putting a WebQuest together is not much different from creating any kind of quality lesson that engages students in the learning process. It requires getting your learners oriented, giving them interesting and achievable tasks, giving them the resources and guidance they need to complete the task, telling them how they will be evaluated, and then summarizing and extending the lesson. These can be thought of as separate building blocks. By changing each of these blocks, you can use this structure to accomplish a wide range of learning goals.

> Putting a WebQuest together is not much different from creating any kind of quality lesson that engages students in the learning process.

Introduction: The purpose of the introduction section of a WebQuest is twofold: to orient the learner as to what is coming and to raise the learner's interest in the topic by a variety of means. It can do this by making the topic seem relevant to the learner's past experience; relevant to the learner's future goals; attractive, interesting, and important because of its global implications; and fun because the learner will be playing a role or creating something.

Task: The task in a WebQuest is a description of what the learner will have done by the end of the exercise. It could be a project like a *PowerPoint* presentation or a *HyperStudio* stack; or it might be a verbal activity, such as being able to explain a specific topic. It is most likely to be a combination of activities.

Process: The process in a WebQuest is where the teacher suggests the steps that learners should go through in completing the task. It may include strategies for dividing the task into subtasks and descriptions of roles to be played or perspectives to be taken by each learner. The instructor can also use this place to provide learning advice, such as how to conduct a brainstorming session. This process description should be relatively short and clear.

Resources: The resources in a WebQuest should be a list of Web pages which the instructor has located, ones that will help the learners accomplish the task. The resources are pre-selected so that the learners can focus their attention on the topic rather than surfing aimlessly. It is important to note that the resources for students are not restricted to those found on the Web. Depending on the roles they are playing, they may be given additional Web sites. By giving separate data sources to learners, you ensure the interdependence of the group and give the learners an incentive to teach each other what they have learned.

Evaluation: The evaluation is an important part of the WebQuest model. If we are going to justify the expense of using the Web for learning, we need to be able to measure results. Since the learning we are looking for is at the loftier reaches of Bloom's Taxonomy, we cannot gauge it readily with a multiple choice test. An evaluation rubric is warranted. The rubric may examine the different aspects of the student product and establish benchmarks for each aspect. It is intended to be printed and given to the evaluators who could be teachers, parents, or peers. Evaluation rubrics would take a different form, depending on the kind of task given to the learner.

Conclusion: The conclusion section of a WebQuest provides an opportunity to summarize the experience, to encourage reflection about the process, to extend and generalize what was learned, or some combination of these. It rounds out the document and provides the reader with a sense of closure. One good use of the conclusion section is to suggest what a teacher might use in whole class discussion to debrief the students about a lesson.

In planning and designing the WebQuest, the teacher's primary job is to provide a workable plan and maintain the structure around which students can successfully work. Once the plan is in place, the teacher will then coach the students as they work and learn side by side.

It is easy to let the technical aspects of Web publishing intimidate you. For example, the use of a WebQuest template can be helpful. Sound planning and organization will be important tasks. Set incremental goals, both short-range and long-range goals so that you can experience success throughout the project. Many beginners set overly ambitious goals and then feel frustrated when they cannot accomplish them all. It is better to have achievable and observable incremental goals.

Another important task is to define all the jobs that need to be done and then assign those jobs to the appropriate people. It is important to match the right people with the right jobs. Questions to consider: Who collects the information? Who does the word processing? Who does the artwork? Who does the scanning and video? Who is the project historian?

> In planning and designing the WebQuest, the teacher's primary job is to provide a workable plan and maintain the structure around which students can successfully work.

Reflection, Evaluation, and Assessment

An effective assessment plan is important to justify time and resources spent on your project. A balanced assessment program uses multiple strategies to demonstrate growth and performance and should be closely correlated to your stated goals. Before beginning an Internet project, it is important to ask:

How will you know if the project was successful?
How will you measure what the students learn?

A standard complaint about many technology projects and multimedia presentations is that students spend too much time tinkering with fonts, graphics, and layouts and not enough time developing the ideas and content of their presentations. One of your primary jobs will be to help students strike a balance between content and presentation and to help them develop the varieties of skills they need to produce meaningful and useful presentations that actually say something.

Assessment strategies can include performance tasks, teacher observations, personal communications, and standardized testing. As Internet-using teachers, we must be able to explain to parents, administrators, and our colleagues what we are doing and to prove to them that this new medium is working as well as our intuition says it is. When we take the time to reflect on our own experiences and those of our students, we can not only answer important questions from our parents and administrators but also make an important contribution to the collected body of wisdom and knowledge in this new medium.

It may be a good idea to include a project background for every Web project published by your students. This page can include information about your project goals and objectives, lesson plans, schedules, project diary, student comments and anecdotes during the process of the project, noteworthy feedback from the community, students' personal evaluations of the project, parental evaluations, and other information which will help to tell the story as an Internet-using teacher.

> **A standard complaint about many technology projects and multimedia presentations is that students spend too much time tinkering with fonts, graphics, and layouts and not enough time developing the ideas and content of their presentations.**

Sample WebQuests to Consider

New Mexico WebQuest: Multidisciplinary; Middle School

Your group works for a brand new businessperson here in Anytown, NM. Mrs. Tamoya is from out of state. She is very interested in New Mexico and is eager to bring her family to live here. She wants members of the company to make suggestions to help her become acquainted with the area. She is assigning a group of you to plan her trips. Since Mrs. Tamoya will be very busy learning about the business for a few months, part of planning her trips requires that you plan her itinerary.

Searching for China WebQuest: Social Studies; High School

The United States government feels very strongly about the need to understand China. To do this effectively, a plenipotentiary is selecting a special team that will travel to China to investigate the country, the people, and the culture. Instead of only sending diplomats, a team is created of people from very different backgrounds, hoping the strategy will give the most accurate and informed perspective. The team members include a foreign investor, a human rights worker, a museum curator or anthropologist, a California state senator, and a religious leader. You and your teammates will create for the American people a special report that makes sense of the complex country that is China.

Let's find out about weather and how it makes a difference all over the world!

Weather Watchers: Science; K–2

What's the weather like today in your part of the world? Do you think it's the same all over the world? No matter where you live, weather is an important part of your life. Let's find out about weather and how it makes a difference all over the world! Pack your bags; we're taking a trip!

Mexico City Earthquake WebQuest: Spanish, Social Studies; High School

The students will be engaged in gathering information related to the subject of earthquakes in general (how they work, safety issues, emergency preparedness, history, etc.) and the Mexico City earthquake specifically. Students will each assume one of the following roles: photojournalist, city planner, emergency volunteer, college student in a collapsed dormitory, news reporter. Working together, the students will design a multi-platform presentation to convey their knowledge about this terrible disaster.

Zelda's Zany Zoo: Science; 3–6

Congratulations! You have just been hired by Zelda the Zookeeper to design a new animal habitat for the city's zoo. The zoo is very run-down, and the visitor count has been decreasing. The city council decided to let Zelda hire consulting teams to design new animal displays. With these new displays, the city hopes to help improve the conditions at the zoo as well as increase the public's interest in seeing animals in realistic habitats. So, get to work!

A Royal Charter from the King: History, Social Studies; Grade 5

Know ye that His Royal Highness, the King of England, has hereby offered his approval to a venture establishing a colony across the seas on the shores of North America. This privilege has been extended to your group contingent providing plans for such a colony. Such plans will, using the best available knowledge, ensure the success of the colony and the health and welfare of the King's subjects.

Art for Sale: Visual Arts; Grades 5–8

Your art brokerage firm has been contacted by a rich entrepreneur. She made millions of dollars developing computer games, but her real interest is art. Currently, she owns a vast European art collection, including pieces by famous artists such as VanGogh, Miro, DaVinci, and Rembrandt. However, her recent travels to the Pacific Northwest have piqued her interest in the cultures of the area. She has decided to add three pieces from that region to her collection. It is your job to research the art of the Tlingit, Haida, Tsimshian, Kwakiutl, and other tribes of the Northwest Coast and to select three pieces to add to her collection.

Musicland Theme Park: Visual and Performing Arts, Music; Grades 5–8

You are a team of theme park designers assigned to build a new music theme park in your city. Musicland will have different "lands" for each of the following musical genres: Musical Theater, Early Jazz (Ragtime, Dixieland, and the Blues), New Jazz (Roaring '20s, Swing, and Be-Bop), Rock and Roll, Country and Folk, and Pop. Each design team must choose a land to develop and make it as realistic as possible. Remember, the more authentic Musicland is, the more tourists it will attract.

Personal Trainer: Health; Grades 8–12

You are a personal trainer employed by Berry's Fitness, the most popular new fitness consulting firm. As part of your job, you provide custom, individualized diet and exercise portfolios for the clients of Berry's fitness. Today, your appointments include four clients, each with different lifestyles and interests: John, Michelle, Kim, and Brian.

The Real Scoop on Tobacco: Health; Grades 5–9

You have been hired by the parents of Icabod, a sixth grade student. They suspect their child of smoking or that he is about to start. He has gone through D.A.R.E. and listened to lectures by parents and teachers. However, he thinks they are all just handing him a line. After all, he sees a lot of adults smoking and figures it really isn't so bad. In fact, he thinks it's pretty cool, but he might listen to you. After all, you are his peer. That's what his parents are counting on. They've hired you to convince him to quit smoking. To do this, you must show your commitment to the fight against youth using

You are a personal trainer employed by Berry's Fitness, the most popular new fitness consulting firm.

tobacco and create a memorable message for him. Do a good job—it could be a matter of life and death!

BioDesigns, Incorporated: A Genetic Engineering Project, Life Science; Grades 10–12

You are part of a four-person genetics engineering team working for BioDesigns, Inc. The president of the company, Ms. Bio, calls a meeting for all engineers. "This company has been losing money steadily for the last 18 months! We haven't had a money-making idea since we invented the seedless watermelon. If we don't have a product on the market within six months, we're going to be out of business." She then further states that your team has to invent a new, revolutionary, money-making and genetically engineered product or start looking for new jobs. Your team members include a geneticist, a biologist, an environmentalist/lawyer, and an economist/ethicist.

Planetary WebQuest: Science; Grades 3–12

You are a member of an international scientific team in charge of the first planetary colony in our solar system. Your team must analyze the different planets and decide which planets to colonize. While there is no right answer, you must give reasons both for why you did choose a particular planet and why you did not choose the other planets.

Alone and Homeless 1933: Social Studies, Language Arts; Grade Six

How does a twelve year old survive for a month on 20 dollars during the Great Depression? Your group will use the resources the teacher provided on the Web, as well as the interviews with your elders to write a diary of those 30 days in St. Louis, Missouri, during the year 1933. Your diary will be posted on the Web, and the Elders (along with anyone else) will be invited to read it and comment. Remember that the imagination is never more powerful than when it feeds directly on raw reality. Make the entries plausible, convincing, moving, disturbing, observant—in short, real.

Concluding Remarks

When you combine student projects, Web publishing, and the communications power of the Internet, your teaching will be transformed. Your classroom walls will tumble down. Your students will interact with real people in the real world, using the same methods and the same tools that people in the real world have been using for years. Learning will become authentic and purposeful. Students will find new meaning in the experiences they have in your classroom. And you and your students will share a new excitement in learning.

> When you combine student projects, Web publishing, and the communications power of the Internet, your teaching will be transformed.

Laws of Telecommunications

- Don't sweat the details!

- Operate on a need-to-know basis.

- The important thing is to begin.

- You will learn what you need to know through experience.

- Don't think you have to be a technological expert or a computer nerd to go online.

- As you explore and gain confidence, you will learn the necessary details.

- If you have a really tough problem, you may want to consult a fifth grader.

- It is amazing that if you have only one password, every student in your class will know it. However, if your students have their own passwords, nobody will know them, not even the students themselves.

- You are most likely even further behind in the Age of the Information Superhighway than you'll ever know you are. Always remember, however, that most people are further behind in the Age of the Information Superhighway than you.

(Marsh, 1995)

Student Safety on the Internet

However, some educators and parents are concerned about the appropriateness of some of the material online.

Importance of Safety for Students

Educators worldwide know that bringing the Internet into the classroom promotes student excellence and breathes new life into the educational experience.

However, some educators and parents are concerned about the appropriateness of some of the material online. They are becoming aware that regulating how Internet connections are used in schools is also as important as getting connected.

Many districts and schools that are online have taken measures to keep inappropriate material out of the school setting. Some use hardware and software controls to limit student and faculty access to certain Internet resources. Sometimes students are permitted to use computers only by appointment and under strict supervision. Some schools track where students go on the Internet electronically or by having them fill out forms.

Yet, in spite of all these efforts, there is no guarantee that a determined user won't find a way to access inappropriate material or misuse his or her time on the Internet.

The media informs everyone of problems encountered online, but what is not evident is that the problems are few. As in all areas of supervision of children, common sense and guidance are often sufficient precaution for using telecommunications.

According to the National Center for Missing and Exploited Children:

"Although there have been some highly publicized cases of abuse involving computers, reported cases are relatively infrequent. There are few risks for children who use online services."

While it is impossible to safeguard or isolate students from everything we don't want them to see, know, or come in contact with, it is also important to provide students with access to the tremendous resources available to them online.

In many activities initiated by educators in schools, it has been found that interactive projects involving students are highly motivating. Students are eager to do specified activities. Oftentimes, they want to go beyond the activities to learn about each other, and problems are minimized when projects are structured and supervised. The supervision includes the delineation of expectations and monitoring of student interaction to assure that expectations are achieved. For example, when e-mail letters come addressed to one student, the letters are shared by the group in order for all to enjoy and learn from the activity. This type of sharing creates an open atmosphere in which students, for the most part, monitor themselves.

The Internet, with its free-form organization, has no one entity to supervise what is published or to monitor actions that take place throughout the Internet. There is no overall governing agency or company responsible for the Internet. Therefore, there are few limits to what can be published. While the Internet has a wealth of resources which are of great value to students, there are areas that are not designed for them. The Internet epitomizes freedom of speech, text, video, graphics, etc. While the majority of information is not dangerous for your students, there are areas that are for adults only.

A teacher would never dream of taking a class on a field trip to a major metropolitan area and just dropping the students off on a random street corner, telling them to have fun and the bus will pick them up at 3:00. A good field trip takes planning, organization, supervision, and good communication. The same standards apply to the Internet.

> **The Internet, with its free-form organization, has no one entity to supervise what is published or to monitor actions that take place throughout the Internet.**

What Is an AUP?

To protect schools and to reassure parents, many schools and school districts create and implement an acceptable use policy or AUP. An AUP is a written agreement signed by students, their parents, and the teacher, which outlines the terms and conditions of appropriate Internet use. An AUP goes in to specific detail regarding acceptable uses, rules of online behavior, and access privileges. Penalties for violation of the policy, including security violations and vandalism, are also included in an acceptable use policy. Anyone using a school's Internet connection may be required to sign an AUP which is kept on file as a legal, binding document.

What's in an AUP?

It is important to explain how students and teachers will access the Internet and how it will be used in the classroom.

An effective AUP may cover several topics. When writing an AUP, the policy should define the Internet and briefly discuss the "netiquette" of the online community. It can't be assumed that parents know about the Internet.

It is important to explain how students and teachers will access the Internet and how it will be used in the classroom. The responsibilities of the students must be included. Parents need to be aware of the potential risks of Internet use, including exposure to objectionable material.

Acceptable use policies should include statements that

- address compliance to state, local, and federal laws.
- outline the limits (if any) of access.
- provide definitions of authorized use and authorized access.
- explain the responsibilities of the student, parent, and teacher/administrator.
- set forth a penalty for not abiding by the rules.
- declare who can grant and revoke privileges of Internet access.
- caution against revealing personal information or establishing face-to-face meetings with other people who are online.
- are followed by signature lines for parent, student, and school representatives.

Examples of responsible Internet use to be included in an AUP are

- to conduct research for school-based projects,
- to explore computer systems,
- to exchange electronic mail, and
- to display a high level of computer ethics.

Examples of inappropriate Internet use may include

- sending and receiving materials that are obscene or offensive.
- employing the network for illegal or commercial purposes.
- using abusive or profane language.
- electronic vandalism of equipment or software.

Examples of consequences of violations of AUPs might include the following:

- Violations will result in the loss of computer privileges for a specified period of time.
- When applicable, law enforcement agencies may be involved.

Spread the Word

The best way to avoid misunderstandings and undue concern about Internet use in the classroom is to communicate with students and parents from the beginning. The reason the policy was created was to be proactive. Introducing the AUP to external audiences before something happens might save you time and stress. It doesn't matter whether the policy is created at the district level or the local level; it is important to spread the word.

Many schools host a technology night to introduce families to the Internet. It can be especially effective to have "net wise" students do the demonstrations rather than the teachers. Teachers and administrators are given the opportunity to meet with the parents to talk about how the Internet will be used in the classroom. The AUP can be explained as well as its ramifications. From the beginning, everyone is clear as to what is allowed and what is not allowed and what will be done to enforce the policy.

Examples of AUPs

There are several online resources that include examples of Internet contracts or acceptable use policies. They include the following:

Child Safety on the Information Highway

This guide for parents has a good example of a simple "Internet Contract."
http://www.4j.lane.edu/safety/

K–12 Acceptable Use Policies

This thorough site by Nancy Willard shows some good acceptable use policy examples.
http://www.erehwon.com/k12aup/

> The best way to avoid misunderstandings and undue concern about Internet use in the classroom is to communicate with students and parents from the beginning.

Newlink AUP Links

This site is a collection of K–12 Acceptable Use Policy resources.
http://www.usoe.k12.ut.us/curr/Internet/aup/aupdir.html

TIES Internet Acceptable Use Policy Links

More AUP information is available from the Technology and Information Educational Services, a computer consortium of 49 school districts in Minnesota.
http://www.ties.k12.mn.us/techplan/policy.html

Filtering Software

Another trend in controlling student access to the inappropriate sites on the Internet is in the form of software which can either block offensive Internet sites or keep track of each step a person has taken while online. Tools are available that restrict access to all areas of the Web that are unsafe for students. When these tools are in place, they will not let students get to those areas, even accidentally.

The biggest risks for students using the Internet include exposure to inappropriate material, potential physical molestation, the danger of providing physical descriptions or arranging face-to-face meetings, and the risk of harassment where students encounter e-mail messages that are harassing, demeaning, or belligerent. Safety solutions for students using the Internet include education, supervision, and software.

There are software programs that function as filters. They work hand in hand with the browsers you use. Filtering software can block different Internet resources, including material from the World Wide Web, electronic mail, newsgroups, mailing lists, FTP, and Telnet. To use the software, the student starts the Internet browser and enters the URL of a Web site. The access software checks a database that contains blacklisted sites and objectionable terms or phrases. Either the Web site appears on the student screen or students receive a "cannot access" message.

Many types of inappropriate information can be filtered. They include information such as the following:

Violence/profanity	Partial nudity
Full nudity	Sexual acts
Gross depictions	Intolerance
Satanic/cults	URLs you add yourself

There are many advantages of using filtering software. Students have limited access to inappropriate data. Sites can be rated by age appropriateness. Passwords can be provided for every user with set graduated levels of access. Programmable timers can be set to limit the amount of online access per day or week or month. Filtering software can prevent credit card numbers, phone numbers, and names and addresses from being sent via e-mail and chat rooms.

There are also some disadvantages of using filtering software. It is difficult to evaluate terms in the context. Sometimes the following topics could not be accessed: sexual harassment research; Anne Sexton's works; breast cancer information; use of marijuana for medical purposes; and others. Since the filtering software uses databases, it is impossible to have every inappropriate URL listed. Filtering software can be costly for a site license. Some of the software requires monthly subscription costs.

Internet filters vary in their monitoring abilities. Their methods for filtering also vary. Some let you customize a list of sites you want filtered out, while others provide a readymade list of such sites, thus making your task easier. You can usually download most filters from the manufacturer's Web site and use the software free for a trial period. Popular filtering software programs include the following, most of which are under $50 but may require monthly update fees.

There are also some disadvantages of using filtering software.

CyberPatrol is the leader in the market. It blocks most objectionable sex sites and some violent content. It is likely to block some sites that don't contain obscene material. It can set the length and the time of day for access.

CyberSnoop is a new product that tracks student access to all Internet resources. It filters out inappropriate sites and shuts down connections if a violation occurs. This is the only software that can filter and display the content of a chat session, e-mail message, and newsgroup posting.

Net Nanny blocks the fewest sites of all products. It does have the ability to add to the list of objectionable sites. It does not access any sites with the word "sex." It can block incoming and outgoing e-mail. It tracks access attempts and blocks software.

SurfWatch is another leader in the market. It blocks inappropriate sites and terms. It can not alter the list of words to be blocked, but sites can be added to the database. It blocks only known sites and does not screen other objectionable material.

Internet Watch Dog is strictly a monitoring software; it does not block any access. It generates a report listing every site visited by the user. It can capture screen shots of any computer activity at predetermined intervals.

CyberSitter blocks offensive sites and violent content. It is best at identifying words in context so as to block phrases and subject-sensitive material. It only blocks URLs, not IP addresses. It can block and alert parents via e-mail.

Remember, these products are only tools to help you monitor your students' activities in cyberspace. Never assume that the filters can take your place in guiding your students and in keeping them out of trouble.

Other Options for Educators

Teachers can frequently review expected behaviors and safety rules. They can practice role-playing situations before students gain access to the Internet. Teachers should always monitor students by locating computers in open, visible areas. Teachers can check student e-mail accounts frequently. They can encourage students to use searching engines and directories which are specifically designed for students, such as Yahooligans! They can strictly enforce their acceptable use policy and punish violators.

Educators can also develop Internet-safe lessons by never starting a lesson by having students use only search engines. Restrict students to only a few sites that you, as the teacher, have previewed. Teachers can develop a work sheet or educational guide with questions students must complete when they visit the assigned site so as to discourage aimless wandering. It is important to require students to find very specific information, not just to surf. It may also be a good idea to have students write down the URL of any site they visit and use.

Another solution to restricting student access to ensure safety is the use of software which will allow you to download entire sites for viewing offline at a later period. Software for this purpose includes *WebBuddy* or *WebWhacker*. This is a good idea also for taking advantage of sites on computers without Internet access.

Education will be the most effective filter. "Software does nothing to prevent kids' access to their own bad judgment," said Larry Magid, a cyber columnist with the *Los Angeles Times*. "The key tool is not going to be embedded in software, but in the minds of children. If you can teach kids now to protect themselves, that's much better than any software tool. It's the software between the ears that counts" (Offutt and Offutt, 1996).

Rules for Online Safety
for Kids

A pamphlet developed jointly by the National Center for Missing and Exploited Children and the Interactive Services Association contains a list of items entitled "My Rules for Online Safety." These rules are written in terms that both parents and children can understand. Here are the rules recommended by the NCMEC:

- I will not give out personal information such as my address, telephone number, parents' work number or address, or the name and location of my school without my parents' permission.

- I will tell my parents right away if I come across any information that makes me feel uncomfortable.

- I will never agree to get together with someone I "meet" online without first checking with my parents. If my parents agree to the meeting, I will be sure that it is in a public place and take my mother or father along.

- I will never send a person my picture or anything else without first checking with my parents.

- I will not respond to any messages that are mean or in any way make me feel uncomfortable. It is not my fault if I get a message like that. If I do, I will tell my parents right away so they can contact the online service.

- I will talk with my parents so that we can set up rules for going online. We will decide upon the time of day I can be online, the length of time I can be online, and the appropriate areas for me to visit. I will not access other areas or break the rules without their permission.

Reprinted from My Rules for Online Safety, *by National Center for Missing and Exploited Children.*

NETIQUETTE AND NETHICS

THE TEN COMMANDMENTS FOR COMPUTER ETHICS (NETHICS) FROM THE COMPUTER ETHICS INSTITUTE

1. Thou shalt not use a computer to harm other people.
2. Thou shalt not interfere with other people's computer work.
3. Thou shalt not snoop around in other people's files.
4. Thou shalt not use a computer to steal.
5. Thou shalt not use a computer to bear false witness.
6. Thou shalt not use or copy software for which you have not paid.
7. Thou shalt not use other people's computer resources without authorization.
8. Thou shalt not appropriate other people's intellectual output.
9. Thou shalt think about the social consequences of the program you write.
10. Thou shalt use a computer in ways that show consideration and respect.

Reprinted from TCM 668 Internet for Teachers & Parents, *Teacher Created Materials,* 1996.

Conclusion

Consider whether the Internet is the best way to accomplish your goals. Sometimes, using paper and pencil, a protractor, a workbook, garden tools, a test tube, and other traditional methods makes more sense. The Internet is like any other classroom resource; there's a right way and a wrong way to use it and a right time and a wrong time. Let the curriculum drive the use of the technology and not the other way around.

> The Internet is like any other classroom resource; there's a right way and a wrong way to use it and a right time and a wrong time.

Management Tips

- Identify and analyze the Internet resources that your students may use.
- List the steps necessary for success. Establish a step-by-step procedure for your students. The more specific you are at the beginning, the better your students will become at navigating on their own.
- Set parameters on time. Consider not only how long completing the project may take but also how much lead time you need to give your collaborators on the Net. Things happen, and sometimes delays can be unavoidable.
- Build in opportunities for feedback. How will you learn when your students are on target and when they are surfing aimlessly?
- Identify how and when students should, can, or must use their fellow students, teachers, and parents as resources.
- Try it yourself first.

- If you are doing a real-time project, don't forget to think about time zones and the cultural differences of the groups with which you are communicating.
- Plan to supplement your Internet activities with a variety of print, video, and computer software resources. The Internet is rich with resources, but it is only one of many tools.
- Always have a backup plan.

Questions to Ask

Some questions to ask when attempting to implement a WebQuest project with your students include the following:

- Is there a real task to do?
- Does the use of the Internet make this task easier?
- Who are you doing this for?
- What do you think telecommunications can do for your students?
- What do you want the outcomes to be?
- What part of your curriculum is most adaptable to the ideas you have?
- Does your project enhance your curriculum?
- Are your goals clear and easy to understand?
- Is your project manageable and simple?
- Are the tasks appropriate for the target audience?
- How much time are you willing to spend on implementation?
- How will you evaluate and assess the project?

Looking Ahead

Though the Internet is relatively new in the school setting, it will soon be commonplace if current growth continues. The educators can prepare for the future now by learning and experimenting with the Internet. The possibilities for the use of the Internet are endless, and it is truly up to the teacher or student to develop creative ways of using it in the classroom. Though it may have some disadvantages, such as expense or time consumed, the Internet can creatively motivate and inspire our students to learn more about their world. The Internet brings the future closer, and we must begin to use and expand its potential whenever possible.

The truth is, nobody knows what lies ahead with the Internet or its technologies, but the future is near. What happens in the next 10 years is difficult to foresee, and what may happen beyond would be foolish to predict.

> The possibilities for the use of the Internet are endless, and it is truly up to the teacher or student to develop creative ways of using it in the classroom.

References

Barron, A. E. (1997). <u>Getting Started with Telecommunications</u>. Tampa, FL: Florida Center for Instructional Technology, University of South Florida.

Buckleitner, W. (1994). <u>Child Safety on the Information Highway</u>. Cupertino, CA: Apple Computer, Inc.

Dockterman, D. A. (1994). <u>Cooperative Learning and Technology</u>. Watertown, MA: Tom Snyder Productions, Inc.

Fisher, C., Dwyer, D. C., and Yocam, K., Editors. (1996). <u>Education and Technology: Reflections on Computing in Classrooms.</u> San Francisco: Apple Press, Jossey-Bass Publishers.

Fraase, M. (1993). <u>The Mac Internet Tour Guide: Cruising the Internet the Easy Way</u>. Chapel Hill, NC: Ventana Press.

Frazier, D. (1996). <u>Internet for Kids</u>. San Francisco, CA: Sybex, Inc.

Gardner, P. (1996). <u>Internet for Teachers and Parents</u>. Westminster, CA: Teacher Created Materials, Inc.

Garfield, G. M. and McDonough, S. (1996). <u>Creating a Technologically Literate Classroom</u>. Westminster, CA: Teacher Created Materials, Inc.

Giagnocavo, G. (1995). <u>Educator's Internet Companion</u>. Lancaster, PA: Wentworth Worldwide Media, Inc.

Global Quest: <u>The Internet in the Classroom</u>. (1993). Videotape, NASA Central Operation of Resources for Educators.

Gorman, M. "The Corruption of Cataloging," <u>Library Journal 120</u> [September 15, 1995]: 34.

Haag, T. (1996). <u>Internet for Kids</u>. Westminster, CA: Teacher Created Materials, Inc.

Harris, J. (1995). <u>Way of the Ferret: Finding Educational Resources on the Internet</u>. Eugene, OR: International Society for Technology in Education.

Hixon, S. and Schrock, K. (1998). <u>Developing Web Pages for School and Classroom</u>. Westminster, CA: Teacher Created Materials, Inc.

Krol, E. (1994). <u>The Whole Internet User's Guide and Catalog</u>, Second Edition. O'Reilly and Associates.

Marsh, M. (1995). <u>Everything You Need to Know About the Information Highway</u>. Palo Alto, CA: Computer Learning Foundation.

Mohta, V.D. (1996). The World Wide Web for Kids and Parents. Foster City, CA: IDG Books Worldwide.

Offutt, E. and Offutt, C. R. (1995). Internet Without Fear. Parsippany, N.J.: Good Apple Press.

Pedersen, T. and Moss, F. (1995). Internet for Kids! A Beginner's Guide to Surfing the Net. New York, NY: Price Stern Sloan, Inc.

Rettig, J. Putting the Squeeze on the Information Firehose: The Need for Neteditors and Netreviewers. *http://www.swem.wm.edu/firehose.html*

Sandholtz, J. H., Ringstaff, C., and Dwyer, D. C. (1997). Teacher with Technology: Creating Student-Centered Classrooms. New York, NY: Teachers College Press, Columbia University.

Schlechty, P. C. (1990). Schools for the 21st Century: Leadership Imperatives for Educational Reform. San Francisco, CA: Jossey-Bass.

Secretary's Commission on Achieving Necessary Skills (SCANS). (July 1991). What Work Requires of Schools: A SCANS Report for America 2000. Washington, DC: U.S. Department of Labor.